THE
LIGHT RAILWAY
ERA
1896 – 1996

John Scott-Morgan

TRANSPORT
Atlantic
PUBLISHERS

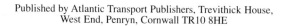

Published by Atlantic Transport Publishers, Trevithick House,
West End, Penryn, Cornwall TR10 8HE

© John Scott-Morgan 1997

ISBN: 0 906899 72 9

Jacket and other supplementary design by Barry C. Lane

Printed by The Amadeus Press Ltd, Huddersfield, West Yorkshire

British Cataloguing in Publication Data
A catalogue record for this book is available from
the British Library

Publisher's note

This book was originally published by David & Charles in two
separate volumes, *The Colonel Stephens Railways* (1978) and
British Independent Light Railways (1980). This combined
edition incorporates a selection of colour photographs.
Although credited to the original photographers where known,
these are all from the Colour-Rail collection, the reference
number being given in each case.

THE
LIGHT RAILWAY
ERA
1896 – 1996

John Scott-Morgan

Atlantic

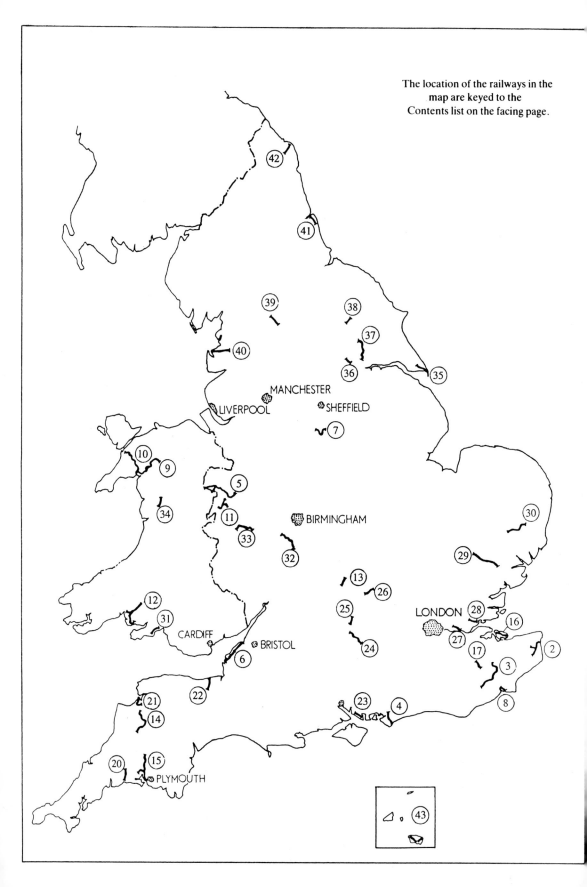

The location of the railways in the
map are keyed to the
Contents list on the facing page.

Contents

Introduction

It is hard to believe that it is almost twenty years since I wrote *The Colonel Stephens Railways* and seventeen years since I prepared *British Independent Light Railways*. Both books have in their own way become classics. *The Colonel Stephens Railways* has been revised and reprinted no less than four times, which has surprised me. There must be a great deal of interest in the Colonel and his empire of light railways.

There are times when I thumb through the pages of collectors' lists from second-hand book shops and am amazed at the silly prices asked for first editions of these books. I hope that this combined edition will make both works available to a whole new group of readers.

We have left the text largely unaltered to keep the original classic feel of both books. However, much has changed since the initial volumes arrived on the bookshelves.

References in chapter 3 to the White Hart at Tenterden should read White Lion. Also, the Rother Valley Railway Company is now trying to rebuild the line back from Robertsbridge to Bodiam. The Tenterden Railway Company, having returned to Northiam from the Wittersham Road direction, now intends to rebuild the line onwards to Bodiam. If all this comes about, it will mean the railway being restored all the way from Robertsbridge Junction to Tenterden Town, a distance of some fourteen miles.

In a similar vein a society has been formed to preserve the last remains of the East Kent Light Railway from Tilmanstone Colliery to Shepherdswell through Golgotha tunnel. Elsewhere, services on the spur from Shrewsbury to Abbey S&M station ended in the early 1980s. The Callington branch still has a basic passenger service as far as Gunnislake, but clay traffic to Marland on the North Devon & Cornwall Junction Railway also ended in the early 1980s.

The Festiniog has now been restored right through from Portmadoc to Blaenau Ffestiniog, and a new company has been formed to rebuild the Welsh Highland Railway. The Burry Port line has recently closed to coal traffic, although there is talk of it being reopened for trains conveying opencast coal. Another casualty has been the Derwent Valley Light Railway.

1996 marked the centenary of the Light Railways Act, which brought into being the majority of standard and narrow gauge light railways. A century on, the light railways of yesteryear have in the main given way to the preservation movement. In most cases the legislation of the 1896 Act was used to transfer legal status from British Railways to the privately-owned preserved lines. The Act has now been replaced by recent legislation with provision for building new railways and also rebuilding on old trackbeds.

January 1997   **John Scott-Morgan**

Above: Class A 4-4-0T No L45 (Metropolitan Railway No 23) at Neasden shed in 1938. This locomotive was the regular motive power on the Brill Tramway until the line's closure in 1935. It is now preserved at the London Transport Museum at Covent Garden. (*LT1*)

Below: Last days on the Swansea & Mumbles Railway. Car No 1 at Oystermouth station in March 1959 shortly before closure of the line at the end of the year. (*E.S. Russell - IR54*)

Above: Cleobury Mortimer & Ditton Priors Light Railway. 0-6-0PT No 2144, with spark-arrester chimney, at Cleobury Mortimer on a special in May 1955. (*E.S. Russell - BRW238*)

Below: Shellhaven station on the Corringham Light Railway, April 1939. An Avonside 0-6-0ST is coupled to a four-wheel ex London, Tilbury & Southend Railway carriage. (*The Pendragon Collection - IR299*)

Part 1

THE
COLONEL STEPHENS
RAILWAYS

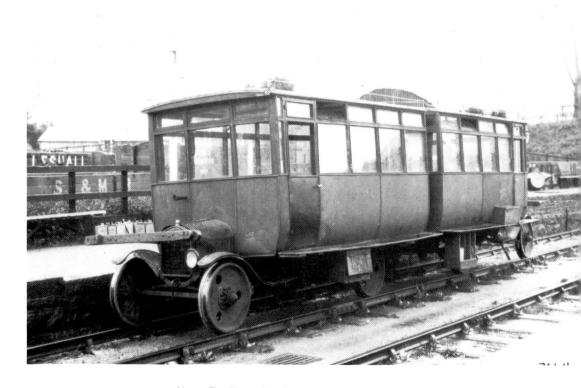

Above: The Shropshire & Montgomeryshire Railway, like one or two other Colonel Stephens' lines made use of railbus sets, one of which is seen here at Kinnerley in 1926. (*LPC courtesy Ian Allan*)

The Colonel and his Railways

In the closing years of the last century, after the 1896 Light Railways Act had been passed, there emerged a number of light railways of various gauges. Among these largely rural lines was a group of light railways which in later years became known to many as the Colonel Stephens railways. All were managed by Colonel H. F. Stephens from an office at Tonbridge, Kent. However, not all had been built by the Colonel or his team at Tonbridge; some lines, the Weston, Clevedon & Portishead, and the Festiniog, among them, were acquired under a management contract over the years. For all their historical technicalities they had one basic thing in common and that was their profit, or lack of it. Most of the light railways managed by Stephens were stony broke and made no bones about the fact. The lines were managed on an elastic-band-and-string economy that would make a modern day economist smile.

To date little is known of the private life of Colonel Stephens because most of the historical data, plans, and photographs of proposed and constructed lines were destroyed at nationalisation in 1948 by the then manager of the Group, W. H. Austen and his office staff at Tonbridge; but from the items that survived to the present day we get just a glimmer of the man's character and achievements.

Holman Frederick Stephens was born in Hammersmith, London on 31 October 1868. His father, Frederick George Stephens was well known for his membership of the pre-Raphaelite Brotherhood. However, unlike his father, young 'Holly' showed little or no interest in following in his father's footsteps. Even from an early age young Stephens had an interest in railways. One early account goes that an old lady, who used to be friendly with the Stephens family, could well remember young Stephens sitting on the floor of his nursery surrounded by track and primitive model rolling stock.

Stephens attended University College School and was also educated on the Continent before he matriculated from London University in 1887, where he had studied civil engineering under Sir Alexander Kennedy. He joined the Metropolitan Railway at Neasden and worked under J. J. Hanbury from 1889 to 1890, but then Stephens embarked on a career of building and managing light and heavy railways up and down the country. His first project was the Paddockwood & Hawkhurst Railway which was opened in stages during 1892 and 1893. Stephens was only 22 at the time, a very young age for the responsibility of building a railway. It was with the Paddockwood line that the features epitomised in the light railways built by Stephens in later years emerged; the steep gradients, corrugated iron buildings, sharp curves and numerous level crossings.

The next line for which Stephens was responsible was the 3ft gauge Rye & Camber Tramway, built without a statutory order of any kind on private land and opened in 1895. Stephens designed an internal combustion locomotive for this line to the Akroyd Stewart principle. The machine was never built but later Stephens experimented with a number of variations of petrol and diesel traction on his other lines. This was followed by the construction, again on private land without an order, of the Selsey Tramway in 1897. Later the line obtained a measure of legality when in 1915 a Light Railway Order was issued by the Board of Trade.

During the 1900s an office was opened in Salford Terrace, Tonbridge, from which all of the Colonel's lines were managed. It was during this period in the early years of this century that most of his lines were constructed. The Light Railways Act of 1896 helped greatly in this field. A summary runs as follows:

1898   Order for the Rother Valley Railway, later the Kent & East Sussex Light Railway
1900   Order for the Isle of Sheppey Light Railway
1904   Bere Alston & Callington Railway (which incorporated the 3ft 6in gauge East Cornwall Mineral Railway; became part of the Plymouth, Devonport & South Western Junction Railway)

Holman Frederick Stephens; 1868-1931.

Former LBSCR A1X 0-6-0T No 2 *Portishead* seen here with a train of ex-LSWR four-wheelers at Portishead in 1938 awaiting the road to Clevedon. The WC&PR purchased two LBSCR A1X 0-6-0Ts from the Southern Railway, the first in 1926, becoming No 2 *Portishead*. A second engine was bought in 1937 and became No 4. Later both locomotives were taken into GWR stock, becoming Nos 5 and 6. No 5 survived until 1954 in store at Swindon Works.

Photomatic/Ivor Gotheridge collection

1909   Reconstruction of the Burry Port & Gwendraeth Valley Railway

1910   The Potteries, Shrewsbury & North Wales reconstruction and metamorphosis into the Shropshire & Montgomeryshire Light Railway

1911   East Kent Light Railway

In the same year he also took over the Weston, Clevedon, & Portishead Light Railway from G. S. Newton who in that year emigrated to Canada. After war service in Britain, between 1914 and 1916. when he was given the rank of Lt Colonel, Royal Engineers (TR). In 1920 he promoted the Edge Hill Light Railway. In 1922 Stephens was responsible for building the North Devon & Cornwall Junction Railway, and for taking over the Snailbeach District Railways. In 1922 he was also responsible for the Ashover Light Railway. In 1923 Stephens was offered the chance of grouping his lines into the Big Four. He declined, preferring to remain independent.

After 1923 he was made consultant engineer for the Welsh Highland Light Railway and later the Festiniog; then he was made chairman and managing director of both concerns by the shareholders. This move did not make the workers on both concerns very happy. From the terse correspondence and memos it was clear that Stephens had little time for the Celts on either line, especially those who worked at Boston Lodge works on the FR.

During the latter years of the 1920s Stephens put forward schemes for Light Railways up and down the country; most were to get no further than the drawing board, for example proposed lines like the Isle of Lewis Light Railway and the Surrey & Sussex Light Railway. One line that nearly made it was the Southern Heights Light Railway which was to run between the Southern stations at Orpington and Riddlesdown in Kent. It had the backing of Sir Herbert Walker and the Southern Railway Board. The Southern even put the line firmly on the map by showing it on SR network maps in carriage compartments. The Southern Heights was to be financed with American money and was to have been worked electrically. At the eleventh hour the scheme fell through for two reasons, first the passing of the Transport Act (London) in 1928, which had the preliminary effect of streamlining transport in and around London which made the line surplus to requirements, and second, opposition from the local councils at both towns. Both factors helped to destroy the scheme. It also contributed to the hastening of the Colonel's death which followed after a number of strokes on 23 October 1931 when he was 63.

He owned several properties. In addition to the family home in Hammersmith he owned a house in Tonbridge and rented rooms at Robertsbridge and Dover. He often stayed at The White Hart, Tenterden when visiting the K&ESR. He also belonged to a number of London clubs and professional institutions. His only interest apart from railways appears to have been classical Greek and Roman mythology. This comes out in the names given to locomotives on his various lines, names like *Juno, Dido, Hesperus, Hecate.*

He will also always be remembered for his petrol railbuses and railcars. However, few people realise the prototype was in fact a Wolseley Sidley chassis which was on trial as a rail lorry on the K&ESR before going to the Selsey Tramway as an early petrol railcar.

After his death in 1931 his lines slowly declined into bankruptcy and closure, and a new boss had taken charge of the group, W. H. Austen, who had been a friend and partner of Stephens from the days of the Paddockwood project. Austen was to manage what remained of the group until the government take-over with nationalisation of railways in 1948, after which most of what was left was slowly closed down.

Today little remains of this empire of minor lines. The Southern Region still operates a short section of the East Kent Railway as far as Tilmanstone Pit. Part of the Kent & East Sussex is being restored by a preservation society, and the Festiniog Railway has nearly been fully restored. The Plymouth, Devonport & South Western Junction still carries a BR passenger service between Bere Alston and Gunnislake.

The Colonel and his empire of minor lines have been steeped in mystery and the subjects of many tall stories. This album, it is hoped, reveals something of the truth of the life and works of one of the most fascinating administrators in Britain's railway history.

Above: Ashover Light Railway's Baldwin-built 4-6-0T *Joan* at Ashover Butts in June 1947 with an SLS special. At this time the line was on the brink of closure as can be seen by the state of the stock. (*J.M. Jarvis - NG68*)

Below: North Devon & Cornwall Junction Railway, opened in 1925 and the last standard-gauge line to be built by Colonel Stephens. 2MT 2-6-2T No 41216 and a single Bulleid Brake 3rd were at Hatherleigh station on a Halwill to Torrington train in July 1964. (*T.J. Edgington — BRS774*)

Above: WD Austerity 0-6-0ST No 188 and train at Kinnerley on an SLS tour of the Shropshire & Montgomeryshire system in 1959, only a year before closure. (*WD19*)

Below: Ex Plymouth, Devonport & South Western Junction Railway 0-6-2T No 30758 *Lord St Levan* at Eastleigh after withdrawal, c 1957. This locomotive was the less photographed of the company's two 0-6-2Ts. (*K. Cooper -BRS496*)

1 THE RAILWAYS AND THEIR ATMOSPHERE

A tribute to the rural folk who lived on the various Colonel Stephens' Light Railways

The Colonel Stephens' Light Railways: what were they really like? Looking back over the years, through the mists of time, one can imagine the early days of most of the railways managed by the Colonel, before the days of the motor bus and lorry.

The railways he managed possessed something that the main line railway could never hope to have. Indeed the Colonel Stephens' railways had a deeply human spirit that lacked the humbug and hypocrisy of the railway rule book, deeper rooted than any railway official could ever hope to understand, for the world of the large companies was the world of the timetable and the express, of the heavy fitted freight and the suburban train bustling its way from main line terminal to the outer suburbs.

In contrasts from the far north of Wales to the rolling downland of South East England, the Colonel's little rural lines ran between the hills and over the streams and rivers, onward their journey went, often from nowhere to nowhere. They went through some of the most beautiful country that Britain could offer, and as the trains passed along their timeless path, from little stations and sleeper-built halts from dawn to dusk, they seemed to take with them the hopes and the dreams of the country folk they served so well, the same local folk who manned the stations, maintained the track, repaired the fences and operated the trains. Most were village folk, coming from the rural areas through which the Colonel's many light railways ran. They knew a peace and tranquillity so very far from our world of industrialists and trades unionists, for theirs was a world where demarcation did not exist.

The station masters and porters of these country stations were some of the last freemen of Britain, for in most cases they were their own bosses and it was entirely up to them how the railway ran. Not for them was it necessary to refer to higher authority to hold connections at junctions. Moreover, not only did they run their stations smoothly and efficiently, but also

somehow found time in their day to tend the flowers in the station garden or give a polite piece of advice to any stranger visiting their domain, so unlike the station staff of many of the stations on today's ultra-modern railway system.

Only a man like Stephens could possibly have run these lines, for he was more than a mere railway engineer or promoter, and so much more than a general manager or organiser. Like an emperor he ruled his empire from his office in Salford Terrace, Tonbridge. His domain stretched far and wide, and his concept of railway operation seemed to exist throughout his light railway kingdom. All the colonies in Stephens' domain seemed to have a great measure of individuality and independence, for although they all had much in common all seemed to have so much individual character in themselves. No two were really alike, and all offered so much to the transport historian and enthusiast who took the trouble to venture off the beaten track to the Rolvendens and Kinnerleys of this rural world. Such a trip would take one almost out of reality and into a time where people were individualists and society valued each and every member by what he stood for in himself, rather than by sheer materialism. One felt almost privileged to be there, but the people of the Kentish Weald and the Welsh Border Country were a friendly crowd, people who in the main one could trust and make friends with. As the train rumbled and bucketed its way through the darkening evening sky, as the gas lamp flickered, casting long dark shadows down the carriage compartment walls, and as the steam of the little Emmett-like locomotive plumed skywards in puffs of pure white vapour, one had a feeling of great contentment, for the day's work was done, and it was time to return to nowhere, from whence one had come that morning.

But then came a war—the second great conflict—and after it was over and all had returned to peace, nothing was ever quite the

same again, for much had been lost and destroyed and people's hearts were hardened and changed. Even in the 1930s buses had already begun to displace rail services on the grounds that they were more flexible, more economic and better suited to the needs of rural communities. One by one the Stephens lines closed. After the war the pace quickened. Then came the Beeching Plan when legislation was used as an excuse to close as many rural railways as possible, regardless of whether these same lines made a profit or not, and regardless of whether the local country folk had an adequate bus service. Today many rural areas including many served by Stephens railways are totally without public transport.

The Paddock Wood & Hawkhurst Railway in its last years, one of several Southern Region branches in East Sussex and Kent closed to passengers during the 1950s and 1960s. Class H 0-4-4T No 31519 leaves Paddock Wood for Hawkhurst in the summer of 1959.
G. M. Kichenside

Below:
Opening day on the S&M with former LSWR 0-6-0 *Hesperus* and train of ex-works Midland bogie carriages posing for a photograph at Meole Brace. The locomotive is seen here in immaculate blue livery. A number of locomotives were painted red for a time. The vehicle behind the locomotive is a Midland four-wheeled parcels full brake. This vehicle was used long after the end of passenger services, often as a brake van.
LPC Ian Allan

The Plymouth, Devonport & South Western Junction Railway still operates as far as Gunnislake as a basic railway, in almost modern Stephens form. These four views capture its unique atmosphere.

Above: Callington terminus on a Sunday in July 1962, with 2MT 2-6-2T No. 41216 on shed awaiting the resumption of services the following day. The line was cut back to Gunnislake in 1966.
(*Tommy Tomalin - BRS870*)

Left: 2MT No. 41316 arrives at Callington with its train from Bere Alston in June 1962. Beyond the station's overall roof can be seen the locomotive shed. (*P.A. Fry - BRS776*)

Above: Ex London & South Western Railway 02 0-4-4T
No 30183 heads a train of vintage bogie stock across
Calstock viaduct, September 1955.
(*J.M. Jarvis - BRS561*)

Below: 2MT No 41302 on a pick-up goods near Luckett
Hill on its way to Callington, April 1960. (*BRS893*)

Above: The Selsey Light Railway, with Manning Wardle 0-6-0ST *Morous* arriving at Selsey station with a train in the 1930s. (*J. E. Kite*)

Below: One of Colonel Stephens' narrow gauge lines was the Ashover Light Railway. A Baldwin 4-6-0T is seen at Ashover Butts in the early 1920s. (*Real Photographs*)

2 THE EAST KENT RAILWAY

The East Kent Railway was perhaps the Colonel's most disappointing venture, as far as the lines that materialised were concerned. It was promoted shortly before the first world war to serve the newly discovered East Kent coalfield, which extended underground from the Dover and Deal areas of Kent out to sea under the bed of the English Channel.

Many of the mines built were never opened, and much of the machinery was left on the surface to rot. The promotion of the light railway to serve the mines in the district was started in 1910, and at a meeting held in Canterbury between the Light Railway Commissioners and the promoters on 17 and 18 October 1910 the Commissioners gave their approval to the scheme to build the line. On 19 June 1911, a Light Railway Order was granted together with approval from the Ministry to build several extension lines to collieries along the route.

From the beginning the line was designed to

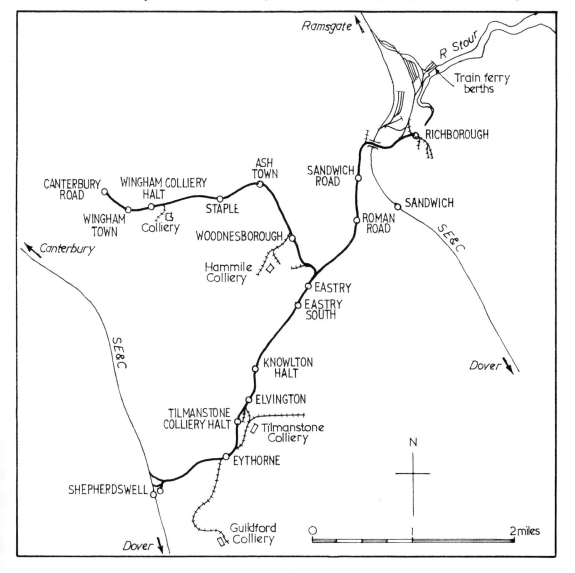

Above: East Kent Railway No 2 at Shepherdswell in immaculate olive green, April 1939. This locomotive was originally Weston, Clevedon & Portishead Railway *Walton Park*. She was later sold for use in industry where she was renamed *Winston Churchill*. (*R.G. Jarvis - SR43*)

Below: At the same location and on the same day, class 0 No 6 is in Southern Railway experimental sage green. This livery was only applied to a small number of locomotives in the late 1930s before the lighter olive green was adopted as standard. (*R.G. Jarvis - SR44*)

The opening of the East Kent Railway in November 1912, showing the official party before the opening ceremony. The locomotive is ex-Whitland & Cardigan 0-6-0ST No 2, later GWR No 1386 (EKR No 1) and the carriage behind is the K&ESR Hurst Nelson bogie brake third. *W. H. Austen collection TRC*

serve the collieries and passenger traffic had to take second place in priorities. The contractors built a temporary pilot line from Shepherdswell on the SECR Canterbury-Dover line, to Tilmanstone Colliery in early 1912. The temporary line went around Golgotha Hill and later, when a double track tunnel was bored through the hill, the temporary line was removed. Although Golgotha tunnel was built for double track only one track was laid, and much of the hard chalk mined out of the second portion of the tunnel was neatly stacked in blocks along the second alignment. The first sections of the new railway from Shepherdswell to Wingham colliery and the branches to the colliery at Tilmanstone, Guildford, Hammill and Staple were opened in November 1912.

The Company had plans to build a line to Canterbury City from Wingham but although it had a Light Railway Order, and had surveyed the proposed route, the scheme got no further than Canterbury Road, a station only a mile from Wingham Colliery. The Canterbury extension to Wingham, along with the extended lines from Eastry to Sandwich Road were opened in 1925. Other parts of the line between Shepherdswell, Eastry and Wingham Colliery had been opened to passenger traffic on 16 October 1916.

During the first world war, the War Department developed Richborough Harbour as a staging point for sending stores and heavy equipment over to the forces in France. After the Armistice in August 1918 the harbour was virtually out of use. Colonel Stephens envisaged a great new port at Richborough, with cross-channel services and plenty of outside trade. The Colonel promoted a line from Sandwich Road to Richborough Harbour which, along with the rest of the branch from Eastry, opened in 1925.

Stations were constructed at Poison Cross and Roman Road to serve the lower part of the Richborough branch. A platform was built at Richborough by the Company in the expectation of operating passenger trains north of Sandwich Road, although no passenger trains were ever run over this section of the branch.

The station buildings along the line were very primitive, even by Colonel Stephens' standards. Most were wooden huts without running water or electric light and a number had no lavatory. Apart from the coal traffic the line handled local farm produce but very few passengers. The train service which operated up the line from Shepherdswell to both of the branches discouraged any would-be passengers because of its infrequency. The passenger service between Eastry and Sandwich Road was finally suspended on 31 October 1928. It is a wonder the Company at this time did not consider closing the rest of the system to passenger traffic.

The EKR had quite a collection of locomotives and rolling stock which were repaired and overhauled in the workshop at Shepherdswell. At the time of opening in November 1912, the EKR owned an ex-GWR saddle tank, No 1386 as EKR No 1, plus a selection of open wagons, and the K&ESR bogie Pickering brake which was, at this time, used only for inspection work.

The East Kent ordered a new Hawthorn 0-6-0T similar in design to *A. S. Harris*, on the PD&SWJR. The order was placed shortly before the outbreak of the first world war but the engine was sent to the WD, presumably in France, when completed.

Compensation was paid with a Kerr Stuart 0-6-0T, which was sold at cut price to the EKR in 1914. The mainstay of motive power on the line was in the form of SE&CR O1 0-6-0s, although shortly after the war the line acquired two former LSWR tank locomotives. One was the Adams 4-4-2 radial tank and the other the Beattie 0-6-0 saddle tank. In 1916, when passenger trains were introduced, the East Kent acquired an LSWR unrebuilt 'Ilfracombe goods' 0-6-0 locomotive. Presumably this old-timer was purchased because there was nothing else available. The line also had locomotives on loan from the K&ESR from time to time and both *Northiam* and *Hecate* worked on the EKR at different times in their lives.

The carriage stock consisted of vehicles of LSWR, LC&DR and NLR origin, mostly four- and six-wheelers. In 1945, two LSWR brake thirds were purchased from the Southern Railway, to replace most of the old carriage stock already described.

Most of the goods vehicles used over the line belonged to other main line railway companies, but the EKR had a small fleet of open wagons, mostly used for internal work.

The line managed to carry on through the depression and up to the years before the outbreak of the second world war, during which traffic began to pick up again because of the increased output from the coalfield and the WD also operated rail-mounted guns on the railway; but after the war was over traffic decreased again and the line returned to its pre-war state of quiet inactivity.

Like so many of the Colonel's railways, the East Kent has its tales, some tall, some true. One that comes readily to mind involved a Saturday afternoon train in the autumn of 1945. The train was headed by one of the O1 0-6-0s and consisted of a single bogie brake carriage and a string of empty open wagons plus a brake van bound for Wingham Colliery. The train left Shepherdswell 10 minutes late and proceeded through Golgotha Tunnel and up past Elvington Halt at a somewhat leisurely pace. On arrival at Knowlton Halt, a friend of mine flagged the train down and duly got on. With a lurch the train started again and wended its way towards Eastry. As the train approached Eastry South a fat gentleman came into view, standing by a boundary fence.

The old boy, probably a local fruit farmer, put his hand out, as if trying to stop a bus; by his feet stood four or five baskets of farm produce for market; but instead of stopping as the country gentleman undoubtedly thought it

No 6 and train bound for Shepherdswell near Eastry in 1932. The embankments along this section seem to be made from ash and slack. The carriage on the end of the train is one of the Kent & East Sussex Pickering bogie vehicles.   *I. Gotheridge collection*

Left:
Eastry station on the East Kent Railway, looking towards the junction of the Canterbury Road branch curving away to the left and the Sandwich Road line going straight ahead, photographed in 1935.
C. R. L. Coles

would, the train continued its leisurely pace past him, despite his screams of abuse and scorn.

After reaching Wingham Colliery where the locomotive disappeared for half an hour to shunt wagons, the train continued to Canterbury Road, where a very strange thing happened. Instead of the locomotive running round the train, as in the normal railway sense, the locomotive, after reaching the level crossing just ahead of Canterbury Road Station, stopped, uncoupled and ran over the crossing to the station and the carriage, which was just in front of a set of points leading to a siding, was levered into motion with the aid of an iron bar carried in the brake van. After the vehicle had been manoeuvred off the main line, the locomotive made its triumphant return, coupled on to the carriage, and started back for Shepherdswell. Any passenger wanting to get off at Canterbury Road was generally ushered down by way of a ladder or porter's barrow, used as a ladder to the ground at Canterbury Road siding.

As the train worked its way home, around the curve just north of Wingham Town (which was constructed of straight rail laid end to end to form a gradual curve) and past the stations at Wingham Town and Eastry, it came presently to the place where earlier on that very afternoon they had left behind a passenger.

Some two and half hours had passed since the last meeting of the two parties concerned and by now the fat farmer had equipped himself with plenty of home-grown ammunition in the form of rotten eggs, tomatoes, apples and many things from the farm compost heap.

The locomotive crew's joviality changed to dismay, as the train passed this notable gentleman for not only did he have more abuse for them than he had before, but also to match, he had items of a more penetrating nature which he duly hurled at the driver and fireman, scoring a number of direct hits into the bargain.

After the war the mangement tried to smarten the line up. Most of the work carried out involved repairing buildings and rolling stock, a number of old vehicles were broken up for scrap, and several of the locomotives were laid aside at Shepherdswell pending their fate. In 1946, the Southern Railway re-purchased the Adams radial 4-4-2T for use on the Lyme Regis branch. This engine is now preserved on the Bluebell Railway in Sussex.

In 1947 the railway carried on in spite of the forthcoming nationalisation of railways a year later. On 1 January 1948 the line became part of British Railways and things started changing rapidly, for from 30 October 1948 the passenger service over the Shepherdswell-Canterbury Road section ceased.

The EKR was one of the first lines to lose its passenger service on the new British Railways network. More closures followed on 27 October 1949 when the section between Eastry and Richborough closed. The line above Sandwich Road had been derelict for years and had not seen a train since the early part of world war two, when the Army had a rail-mounted gun on this section.

The last two sections to close to all traffic were from Eastry to Canterbury Road on 25 July 1950 and the line between Eythorne and Eastry which closed on 1 July 1951, leaving only the section from Shepherdswell to Tilmanstone Colliery in use, which it still is today.

Top left:
Shed scene at Shepherdswell in 1936, showing locomotive No 6 with its new boiler and No 4 the Kerr Stuart 0-6-0T. To the left is the PW crane and runner, behind which are the frames and cab of 0-6-0ST No 1, formerly GWR 1386.

Photomatic/I. Gotheridge collection

Above:
Former LSWR Beattie 0-6-0ST, EKR No 7, takes water at Woodnesborough. *L&GRP*

Left:
Line-up of motive power at Shepherdswell in 1931. From left to right are: unrebuilt ex-LSWR 'Ilfracombe goods' 0-6-0 No 3 formerly 394, Kerr Stuart ex-ROD 0-6-0T No 4, 0-6-0ST No 2 from the WC&PR, ex-LSWR 127 No 7, LSWR 4-4-2T No 488 (EKR No 5) in front of which stands O1 0-6-0 No 6. *H. C. Casserley*

Right:
Golgotha Tunnel shortly after its completion in 1912, looking towards Shepherdswell, showing the chalk cutting and the tunnel built to take two tracks. This section of line is still in use today for coal traffic from Tilmanstone Colliery. *W. H. Austen TRC*

A double headed train on the EKR consisting of 0-6-0s No 6 and No 3 near Eastry in the early 1920s. No 3, the unrebuilt 'Ilfracombe goods' purchased from the LSWR in 1916, was withdrawn in the late 1920s. This locomotive cost more to purchase than any of the rebuilt Ilfracombe locomotives used on the other Stephens' lines. *Ken Nunn LCGB*

Canterbury Road Station in 1925, the end of the EKR. Originally it was hoped to extend the line to Canterbury City, some 15 miles away. In the distance can be seen the cutting towards Canterbury which was built but never used. Canterbury Road was only a mile outside Wingham Village. *W. H. Austen collection*

Domeless Stirling 0-6-0 No 6 at Wingham in 1932 with a train of former Midland and LSWR six-wheelers bound for Shepherdswell. No 6 was purchased from the Southern Railway in 1923 as SR 372 and rebuilt with an O1 boiler in 1933. No 6 was fitted with a squat chimney to operate through Tyler Hill tunnel on the Canterbury & Whitstable Railway. *Real Photographs*

The pithead at Tilmanstone in 1914, showing a variety of open wagons belonging to various railway companies and private coal merchants. Note the coal loading hoppers and the Tilmanstone open wagons in the foreground. *W. H. Austen TRC*

Above: Kent & East Sussex Railway No 3 at Rolvenden in September 1947 after being rebuilt to A1X at St Leonards shed four years earlier. She looks very smart in her new coat of malachite green. (*J.M. Jarvis - SR16*)

Below: 0-6-0ST No 4 (ex LSWR E0335) at Ashford Works awaiting overhaul, June 1939. Shortly before World War II, No 4 was exchanged — along with two spare boilers — for *Hecate*, the 0-8-0T which became Southern Railway No 949. It spent most of the rest of its life at Nine Elms, working around Clapham on carriage shunting, before being withdrawn in 1950. (*SR13*)

3   THE ROTHER VALLEY RAILWAY
(Later the Kent & East Sussex Railway)

The Rother Valley Railway started life in 1897, shortly after the 1896 Light Railways Act was passed. The line was the Colonel's fourth project, after the Paddockwood & Hawkhurst line, and his first railway under the new Act. It ran from Robertsbridge in Sussex, on the South Eastern Railway Tonbridge-Hastings line to Tenterden in Kent. The original Tenterden Station was situated at what was later known as Rolvenden, and it was here that the new company built its locomotive shed and repair shops. The railway served the rural agricultural district of the southern Weald, which stretched from the Ashford area of Kent and ran down to the Romney Marsh taking in the Rother Valley with its hop-farming and wheat-growing, to Rye and Pevensey.

The line opened to traffic on 2 April 1900, from Robertsbridge to Tenterden (Rolvenden), and for the opening the Company had purchased two 2-4-0Ts from Hawthorn Leslie of Newcastle-upon-Tyne, Nos 1 (named *Tenterden*, 2420 of 1899) and 2 (named *Northiam*, 2421 of 1899).

In addition to the locomotives the Company ordered a rake of six four-wheeled carriages,

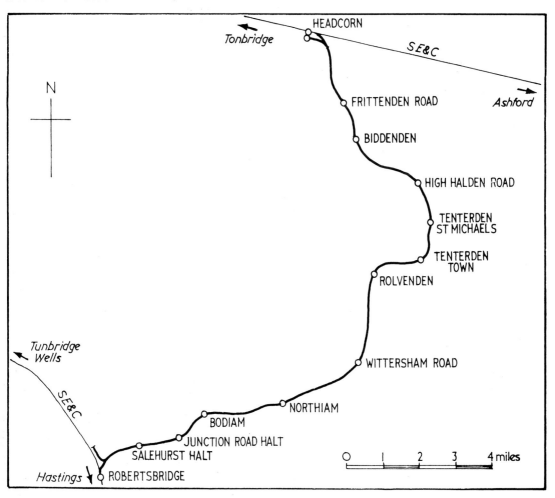

FARMERS' TRAIN

The Kent and East Sussex Line

Ever seen a railway train
wheel deep in the wheat?
Poppies on the boiler dome:
wreaths of meadow-sweet
twined about the driving wheel—
burnished brass and polished steel:
puffs of steam like woolly lambs,
on the line to Bodiam?

His chimney's tall and thin and crowned
with a bell-mouthed top,
brassbound
all round.
He's painted green like new spring grass
and he's always pausing
at the level crossing
to let the farm carts pass.

He sees real trains at Headcorn Halt,
where he's rather shy
as they thunder by
from lordly London to the Coast.
For they're very long
and he's very short,
and he wonders if they give him a thought:
but at Methersham you'll hear him boast
that his very best mate's
the eleven-eight—
the Dover Express that's never late.

But—
as soon as he gets out of sight
of the Main Line with its metals bright
then once again
he becomes THE TRAIN
and there's pride and swank
in every puff, as he goes chuff, chuff,
with a piercing whistle now and then
(Get out of the way, you silly hen)
on his lordly way
to Newenden.

He puffs past farms,
he steams past barns,
to the Biddenden maids he tells tall yarns.
He's a snorting giant
at Freezing Hill,
he whistles the miller
at Northiam Mill,
he puffs the day's news
at the crossing gate
and says what a shame he's
five minutes late!
and snorts of course
it's the Main Line's fault!

He carries grain and he carries hops.
Wherever you hail him, there he Stops!
in fact he's a friendly sort of train.
He takes out shopping farmers' wives:
he carries a load of bees in hives:
and he carries pigs,
and oats
and goats
and several boxes of lollipops
for the village kids
at the village shops.

He knows the Marsh and he knows the Weald,
he knows each wood and he knows each field:
with his bright green paint
and his glistening brass:
the rabbits stop
to see him pass.
And Arcadia's just another station
on his twice-a-daily
pere-
grination!

which were later in 1906 rebuilt into four bogie vehicles. Of the original four-wheeled vehicles Nos 1-4 were all thirds seating 32 passengers each; Nos 5-6 were outwardly very similar to the all thirds, but seated 28 first class passengers, with separate compartments for passengers wishing to smoke.

The Company purchased a small fleet of goods vehicles, which included two dual purpose brake vans and a selection of four-wheeled open wagons numbered 1-10. Later the Company sold most of the original goods rolling stock to the Shropshire & Montgomeryshire and the East Kent railways.

The stations along the line were built of corrugated iron with wooden framing; each station had a station master's office which was also used as a booking office, and a general waiting room. The stations had only gentlemen's outside lavatories and no running water; as if to compensate the stations always seemed to have beautiful gardens with all manner of flowers neatly kept and cared for. The stations at Northiam and Bodiam had loops with a second platform, but in the latter case the loop was later removed.

The line was extended up a 1 in 50 incline to Tenterden Town in 1903, and opened to traffic on 15 April of that year. Tenterden Town station was very different in construction from the other stations on the line, in that it was built of brick; it also had a sizeable general office, from which the line manager could control operations. The general office also had a ticket window at one end where the booking staff worked; the building had at the far end a waiting room and lamp-shed but like the other stations it also only had a gentlemen's lavatory.

On 5 May 1905 the railway was extended to Headcorn on the South Eastern Railway main line from Tonbridge to Ashford. At this time the railway changed its name to the Kent & East Sussex Railway. During this period there were plans for further extensions of the line, the main scheme being to continue from Headcorn to Maidstone, through Sutton Valence. The Maidstone line would have had a very steep incline to the north of Headcorn, where it would have ascended towards the North Downs at Sutton Valence. A number of other more local extensions were planned including lines to Pevensey, Appledore, Cranbrook and Rye, all of which were surveyed but never built.

At this time the Colonel purchased the big Hawthorn 0-8-0T *Hecate* for possible use along the main line from Headcorn to Tonbridge if agreement could be reached with SE&CR. After the Colonel's death in October 1931, Austen wasted no time in exchanging *Hecate* with the Southern Railway for a more useful locomotive, and the bogie carriages were later sold; two went to the Woolmer Instructional Military Railway (later the Longmoor Military Railway) and the third was transferred to the East Kent Railway.

The extension to Headcorn from Tenterden had been built to the standards of the South Eastern Railway, quite unlike the earlier Rother Valley Section. In later years the line was worked in two halves, because of the difference in weight restrictions on the two halves of the railway. The buildings on the Headcorn section were of wood, but similar in appearance to the buildings on the Rother Valley section.

The railway held its own through the first world war and into the 1920s, but it was during this time that the rot began to set in. After the war a vast number of motor lorry chassis became available as Government surplus and these were purchased by quite a few people returning from the war, who went straight into the road haulage business, individually in direct competition with the existing railways. It was bad enough for the main line companies but for lines like the Kent & East Sussex Railway it was almost certain death. The Company managed to make a profit for the first few years of the 1920s, but then began the slide which led to the depression, where the line was handed over to a receiver.

The railway by this time possessed a motley collection of old second-hand ex-main line vehicles. Motive power consisted of nine steam locomotives and one defunct steam railcar, plus three petrol railbus sets, two of which were Fords and one a Shefflex set. These vehicles were conventional Ford road buses on flanged wheels and coupled back-to-back. The conversions for the railbuses were carried out by Edmonds of Thetford. The railbuses drove traffic away rather than encouraging it and the management in Tonbridge was quick to be rid of them soon after the Colonel died.

It was during the mid-1930s that the Company started to hire motive power from the Southern Railway. The locomotives used by the Company were the Southern classes O1 0-6-0, A1X 0-6-0T and P 0-6-0T, although when O1s were not available the SR often sent a Class 0395 0-6-0.

The Company's own motive power was in a desperate situation by this time; of the nine locomotives only three were in working order, the remainder were standing in the dump siding at Rolvenden awaiting their fate.

The carriages were not in a very healthy state either; of the original fleet none of Hurst Nelson vehicles had survived and the Pickering steam railcar, which was used only up to 1912, was thereafter abandoned in a grass grown siding along with a number of vehicles from the North London and London & South Western railways.

However, things were changing at Tonbridge and Mr Austen had started to clear the useless worn-out rolling stock from most of the lines formerly operated by the Colonel; but before the clearance reached the Kent & East Sussex line, an event occurred which should be mentioned— the making of the film *Oh, Mr Porter* with Will Hay and his team. Locomotive No 2 *Northiam*, was patched up and sent via the Southern Railway to Basingstoke for use by the film company on the former Basingstoke & Alton Light Railway. The locomotive was fitted with a tall spiked chimney and given the name of *Gladstone* by the film company. She returned to Rolvenden in the latter part of 1937 and was withdrawn soon afterwards.

At the outbreak of war in September 1939 the KESR passed to Government control. During the first 18 months of the war the line was cleared of all derelict rolling stock and sections of track were relaid with new materials. In 1941 the Army moved in with rail-mounted guns which were stationed at Rolvenden, along with GWR Dean Goods 0-6-0 locomotives to haul them. The Army operated the rail-mounted guns between Rolvenden and Wittersham Road stations from 1941 until 1943 when they were removed. The line played a minor part in the pipeline 'Pluto' plan in connection with the D-Day invasion of occupied France. After the end of the war in 1945 the railway reverted briefly to the Tonbridge management. By this time, however, the writing was firmly on the wall for nearly all the railways in Britain, the Labour Government having pledged in its 1945 manifesto to nationalise the railways along with various other industries.

Mr Austen was not put off by this prospect though, for during the last two years leading to nationalisation the line in many ways was transformed from a run-down affair surviving by hope and charity, to a line which although not financially solvent at least looked a commercial venture.

Above right:

Locomotive No 1 *Tenterden* built by Hawthorn Leslie of Newcastle and train of four-wheelers at Rolvenden Yard in 1900, shortly before the opening of the line. Note the four-wheeled brake van for dual passenger and goods train working. At this time Rolvenden Station was known as Tenterden. Later in 1903, the line was extended up the bank to Tenterden Town, and the lower station became Rolvenden. In the background is the early locomotive shed with locomotive No 2 *Northiam* inside. Later a new brick-and-corrugated iron shed was built to replace the early timber structure.
W. H. Austen collection

Below:
Kent & East Sussex Railway 2-4-0T No 2 *Northiam*, which in the last year or so of its life was immortalised in the classic Will Hay film *Oh, Mr Porter*, for which purpose it was renamed *Gladstone*.   *L&GRP*

Station buildings were smartened up and repainted and in some cases stations were fitted for the first time with electric light, track was relaid with bullhead rail to replace flat bottom rail laid many years before, and concrete fence posts were put in along most of the line from Headcorn to Robertsbridge.

On 1 January 1948 the line passed into the hands of the British Transport Commission which at first made certain improvements to the line, mainly in permanent way. One of the schemes put forward by the new management at Waterloo was to double the track right through from Headcorn to Robertsbridge and to upgrade the track and bridges to allow U and U1 2-6-0 tender locomotives to operate through goods trains along the line.

The plan was dropped as were several other schemes to enlarge goods yards and improve the coal handling facilities. During the second world war locomotive No 3 had been rebuilt. It was in fact the last Terrier rebuilt from A1 to A1X (which involved fitting a later type Marsh boiler with extended smokebox) carried out at St Leonards Depot in 1943. In 1947 it had been sent away to Brighton for a light overhaul and repaint and when it returned to Rolvenden in early 1948 it was resplendent in Bulleid Malachite Green, with the company's initials in an arc over the number on the side tanks.

The locomotive bore its attractive livery for a short time before it was re-painted in plain, unlined British Railways black. The other surviving locomotive 0-6-0ST No 4 had been towed away, along with a collection of rotting carriages and goods vehicles, to Ashford.

During 1949-50 the Southern Region erected new mile posts along the line showing the mileage from Charing Cross. Existing ticket stocks were withdrawn and replaced with the standard British Transport Commission Edmondson card tickets. The line was now operated in two halves, from Headcorn to Tenterden Town and Tenterden Town to Robertsbridge.

The Headcorn section was operated using former SE&CR O1 0-6-0s hauling one brake carriage, normally an SE&CR Birdcage or LSWR corridor brake third, with the occasional train of goods wagons tagged on behind. The Rother Valley section was operated using LBSC A1X class 0-6-0Ts and similar coaches.

By 1953 the line was making a considerable loss and the management at Waterloo decided to close the line to passenger traffic, and keep only the original section from Robertsbridge to Tenterden Town open to goods traffic. The line closed to passenger traffic from 4 January 1954, the last train running on the previous Saturday 2 January. Lifting commenced on the Headcorn extension in mid-1955, and by the winter of that year only the trackless stations and ballast bed remained to show where the line had been.

The remaining goods trains were operated by A1X 0-6-0Ts from St Leonards depot. Operations took the form of one return trip a day, Mondays to Fridays. In 1957 the Southern Region started to use class 03 diesel-mechanical shunters on the line.

In 1958 the Locomotive Club of Great Britain chartered a train over the line from Robertsbridge to Tenterden Town, the first passenger train to Tenterden since closure in 1954, although hop-pickers' trains ran from London to Bodiam and Northiam during the hop-picking season. They were operated using non-corridor birdcage sets and A1Xs. In 1961 came the final closure to all traffic. The LCGB chartered another special train over the line on 12 July 1961; the following day saw the last goods train.

Later in 1961 a preservation society was formed to preserve the line. After a number of setbacks, which included a long legal battle in the high court, the railway was re-opened to traffic on 3 February 1974. The Tenterden Railway Company, the operating authority, is now establishing a Colonel Stephens museum in Tenterden, where it is hoped to exhibit relics from former Colonel Stephens railways.

Arrival at Tenterden in 1939 headed by Southern P Class 0-6-0T and former LSWR bogie brake third bound for Headcorn Junction. By the mid 1930s the K&ESR found that it was short of motive power and therefore had to hire locomotives from the Southern. Among them Brighton A1Xs, SECR Ps, and O1 0-6-0s, and ex-LSWR 0334 0-6-0s made an occasional appearance in the late 1940s. Note the three-arm signal, which controlled both the platforms into the loop and the track to Rolvenden. *Ken Nunn LCGB*

A train at Wittersham Road in 1953, headed by locomotive No 3 *Bodiam*, seen here as BR 32670. Wittersham Road's building was set at right angles to the platform, quite unlike the buildings on the rest of the line. *J. J. Davies collection*

Tenterden Town Station about 1910, showing No 5 *Rolvenden* and train of Pickering bogie stock about to depart for Robertsbridge Junction. At this time Tenterden had three platforms, one main, with buildings, and an island with a bay which can be seen in the photograph. Later the back bay was used for cattle traffic. The island was abandoned in early BR days leaving only the platform with the building in use. Unlike the other KESR stations Tenterden had a brick building.

W. H. Austen collection TRC

A rural scene, indeed, as O1 0-6-0 No 31065 heads a train of a single LSWR bogie brake third towards Headcorn Junction in August 1953, only four months before the Headcorn line closed in 1954. In BR days the O1s and A1Xs were the mainstay of the locomotive fleet on the line, the O1s working the Headcorn Junction-Tenterden section, and the A1Xs from Tenterden to Robertsbridge.

E. C. Griffith

Left:
One of the two former LSWR 0-6-0s owned by the Kent & East Sussex; here No 7 *Rother*, bound for Robertsbridge, pauses at Northiam with an afternoon train composed of GE four-wheel coaches.   *L&GRP*

Bottom left:
Tenterden Town station in the 1920s, with one of the Ford railbus sets standing at the platform.   *L&GRP*

Below:
Shunting outside Headcorn Junction in 1912. Rother Valley ex-LSWR No 0349 was purchased by the company in 1910 and continued in service until about 1935 when she was laid aside at Rolvenden. In 1914 *Juno*, a sister locomotive, was purchased from the LSWR as No 0284. She was also withdrawn at about the same time as *Rother*. Note the water tower and wind pump to draw up water when required, also the train make-up with a number of empty ex-SER tarpaulin wagons from the main line being made up into a train for their return. The locomotive name was painted on the centre splasher but later a cast plate was fitted.
Ken Nunn LCGB

Left:
A Rother Valley Railway Hurst Nelson four-wheel coach in ex-works condition at Rolvenden yard, then called Tenterden, in 1900. The Rother Valley originally had six of these vehicles, later rebuilt by Pickering into bogie vehicles. Note the ornate lettering on the carriage side and the half-tree-trunk sleepers in the background. The Company owned two first and four third class carriages at this time. *W. H. Austen collection*

Right, and right lower:
Two types of point indicator used on the Kent & East Sussex. *L&GRP*

Left:
One of the two former LSWR royal saloons of 1848 at Rolvenden in 1930. After originally being sold by the LSWR this vehicle, along with its sister, ran on the PD&SWJR until the Colonel purchased them in 1905 for use by him as inspection vehicles. However this carriage was occasionally used on ordinary trains as it was for a time the only vehicle on the line with lights for night operation. In 1936 the saloon was purchased by the Southern Railway which intended at that time to set up a railway museum at Eastleigh. After being sent to Ashford for storage, it was later sold as a body to a farm in Kent where it perished in the early 1960s. The second vehicle finished up on the Longmoor Military Railway (see page 42). *H. C. Casserley*

Left:
The Pickering steam railcar of 1905 which is reputed to have worked on the line until 1912, after which it was withdrawn and left to rot until shortly before the outbreak of world war two. The machine had an upright boiler. The chassis is more like a long wheelbase wagon underframe with extra fittings, than an underframe for a steam railcar.

This vehicle was No 16 in the carriage list and later No 6 in the locomotive list. Its underframe still exists as part of the superstructure of Rolvenden water tower. *J. S. Morgan collection*

Locomotive No 2 *Northiam* in Rolvenden shed, August 1933, showing much of the shed interior. Behind No 2 is Terrier tank No 5 *Rolvenden* undergoing a heavy general overhaul. On the right is a pile of fire bricks, and on the floor numerous hoses and bars. This photograph shows the wooden frame construction of the building very well.   *H. C. Casserley*

Kent & East Sussex class A1X 0-6-0T No 3 newly repainted in Malachite Green after the second world war, and seen here with a train in 1947.   *L&GRP*

Locomotives Nos 4 and 8 at Rolvenden Shed in 1935. Both had interesting careers before coming to the Kent & East Sussex Railway. No 4 originally belonged to the LSWR as No 0335. In 1932 it was exchanged by the SR along with two spare boilers in return for *Hecate* the 0-8-0T. It remained in active service until 1948 when she was withdrawn for scrap by BR. No 8 originally belonged to the North Pembroke & Fishguard Railway where she was named *Ringing Rock*, GWR No 1380. Later, on the K&ESR, its name changed to *Hesperus*. It was sold by the GWR to the line in 1914 and withdrawn in 1941.   *H. C. Casserley*

An accident outside Tenterden Town Station in the late 1900s showing 'Ilfracombe goods' 0-6-0 No 7 *Rother* before naming, and a rake of GER four-wheelers. The train was bound for Robertsbridge when the rails spread. Jacks and packing gear can be seen in the foreground. The locomotive and stock were soon righted and returned to service.

W. H. Austen collection TRC

On the heap at Rolvenden in the late 1930s, locomotives *Rother* near left, *Juno* centre, and Terrier *Rolvenden*. At the same time on the other side of the wooden shed, centre of picture, there were a number of ex-NLR and LSWR carriages plus the Shefflex railbus set and the steam railcar. All the junk had been cleared by 1941 when steel prices went up considerably. No 5 was later used to rebuild No 3 *Bodiam* in the late 1930s.
H. C. Casserley

4 THE HUNDRED OF MANHOOD & SELSEY TRAMWAY
(Later the West Sussex Light Railway)

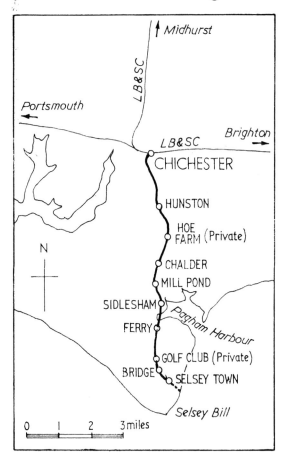

The Hundred of Manhood & Selsey Tramway opened to traffic on 27 August 1897. It ran from Chichester on the LBSCR's Portsmouth-Brighton line, via Pagham Harbour to Selsey. The Tramway was built on private land without a formal parliamentary order, and it was a number of years before any measure of legality was sought.

The Tramway served both local residents and visitors to the area at a time when there was little or no alternative transport. Apart from the tourists the Tramway also served the fishermen of Selsey and farmers along the route to Chichester. Later, after the first world war,

things changed dramatically and with the coming of the motor bus the line lost most of its revenue.

Like most of his lines Colonel Stephens proposed several schemes to extend the Selsey Tramway. In 1913 the Colonel, who was engineer of the line, proposed an extension from Hunston to Birdham, from where two branches would be built, one to East Wittering and the other to West Itchenor. The new line was surveyed in 1913 and powers were granted for its construction, but the outbreak of war in August 1914 stopped the project and it was not resumed.

The buildings along the line were constructed of corrugated iron, but unlike most of the other lines operated by the Colonel, they were smaller, normally one room affairs. Not all stations had buildings and some had only small shelters.

The Company had a strange collection of locomotives and rolling stock, mostly second and third hand. Like so many other Colonel Stephens' lines the Selsey had started with some new rolling stock, consisting of a 2-4-2T built by Peckett of Bristol in 1897, works number 681 and named *Selsey*. This, together with a rake of Falcon bogie carriages, represented the only new rolling stock the Company owned for some years.

During the Tramway's construction, the contractor had used a rather ancient saddle tank locomotive, built by Longbottom Railway Foundry in 1847 for the GWR. This locomotive was later purchased by the Tramway Company and named *Chichester*, after being rebuilt as an 0-4-2ST.

Most of the other locomotives were Manning Wardle saddle tanks purchased from contractors, although there were two exceptions, *Hesperus* from the PDSWJR, and the second *Chichester*, a Hudswell Clark engine which came from Naylor Bros, later the contractors for the Wembley Exhibition. One of the Manning Wardle tanks purchased, *Morous*, came to the line via the Stratford on Avon & Midland

Junction and the Shropshire & Montgomery-shire Railway.

During the early 1920s the Colonel introduced his petrol railbuses to the line, the first of which was the prototype of all his railbuses—the Wolseley Sidley vehicle, built on a chassis purchased after the first world war, with a body built in Maidstone. The Wolseley Sidley was used for trials on the line, and later put into normal service.

The railcar was operated on the line coupled to a Ford road lorry, but occasionally the unit was turned. This was done at Chichester, on the Southern turntable. One morning the car was being turned when the rear portion of the vehicle, which like the front unit, had a radiator, struck a steel post by the side of the turntable and was damaged beyond repair. As it was not a great success the unit was withdrawn. The railcar was later taken to Kinnerley on the S&M where the body was used to refurbish the former LCC tramcar for *Gazelle*.

Not long after the accident the Ford set arrived in 1923. Later, in 1928, this was joined by a Shefflex set. The railcars often trailed a luggage trolley behind them on their journey from Selsey to Chichester and occasionally the trolleys were used by the permanent way department for track ballast. The other carriage stock consisted of former Lambourn Valley and LC&DR vehicles. The Company also had a small fleet of open wagons and vans. One of the former Rother Valley brake vans was used on the line.

The Tramway had an uneventful career through the first world war, but during the 1920s things began to liven up for a time. On

The first locomotive, named *Chichester,* also the contractor's locomotive for the line, is seen here being towed along the road near Hunston in 1897 before the line was opened. The need for this feat arose when the locomotive was needed on the lower section, but was at work on the upper part. This was before the canal bridge was built and the only way was to haul the engine along the road behind the traction engine. Temporary rails were laid in front of the engine and taken up behind. The locomotive, an 0-6-0ST, has had its rear coupling rods removed and is technically running as an 0-4-2ST. After the line opened in August 1897 it was properly rebuilt as an 0-4-2ST using a small pair of trailing wheels.   *E. C. Griffith collection*

3 September 1923, there occurred the worst accident in the Tramway's history. Accidents had occurred on the Tramway over the years before this, but all previous accidents were minor compared with what happened that day.

The 8.15 a.m. tram from Selsey to Chichester, hauled by the second locomotive named *Chichester*, lurched off the track near Golf Club Halt, killing the fireman and badly injuring the driver. None of the passengers on the train were hurt though. The line was closed for two days as a result of the accident. One result was that the Colonel and his management were blamed for negligence, for it appeared that this stretch of tramway had not been relaid for many years and the sleepers were completely rotten.

In 1924 the Tramway took a step towards legality, when an order under the Railway Construction Facilities Act, was granted, which allowed a new company to be formed. This was empowered to take over the HM&ST and all its assets. From January 1924 the Company was known as the West Sussex Railway.

During the 1920s and early 1930s the

Tramway declined and no improvements were carried out. The decline mainly arose from competition by new bus services operating between Chichester and the outlying districts, and as the Tramway was noted for being very slow, people quickly changed their mode of transport when buses appeared on the scene.

In 1924 the Company's finances were in such a mess that the concern could not afford to pay its debentures and several writs were taken out against it. It was after a number of cases had been heard that the high court placed a receiver in charge of matters and the end was in sight. Several offers were made for the line, one from Sir Herbert Walker, General Manager of the Southern Railway, who wished to reconstruct the line as an extension of his electrified system. An alternative offer was made by Henry Greenly, who at the time was looking for a suitable location for a miniature railway for Captain Howey. Later a more convenient site was found for him on the Kent coast between New Romney and Hythe.

By 1934 it was obvious that the Tramway had but a little time to go, a number of the locomotives were out of use and both passenger and goods rolling stock was in a deplorable state. Worst of all, the permanent way was so badly worn in places that the original contractors' rail had been reduced from 41 lb/yd to 25 lb/yd. On 19 January 1935, notices were posted, informing the travelling public that the Tramway was at last closing. It was on that evening that the last train ran from Selsey to Chichester.

The Tramway operated for a week after passenger closures, to clear goods traffic and bring items of rolling stock up from Selsey shed in readiness for the forthcoming sale.

No official order was made by the Ministry of Transport to abandon the line. At the sale that followed all the locomotives and rolling stock went for scrap. Some of the items sold were in fact the property of the Colonel himself and the money from the sale of these items went to his executors.

A number of carriage and van bodies could still be found in the Chichester area until fairly recently. The Tramway was lifted during 1936, although a number of buildings and other structures remained for a number of years after closure.

The Tramway was greatly loved by locals and enthusiasts alike, and as always, with these lines there were some amusing tales told about it. One true story involved the first *Chichester* when the Tramway was under construction. The contractors' locomotive which was at the time working on the northern part of the Tramway was needed for construction work on the southern part of the line. The lifting bridge over the canal at Hunston had not then been completed. Because of the gap the locomotive had to be towed behind a traction engine along the road to the site of Hunston Station. A gang of navvies laid rails in front and retrieved them behind, as the machine was towed along.

The Tramway also had its nickname, some called it the Tram, some the Selsey Bumper, but others at the Colonel's office in Tonbridge called it the Death Trap! In the late 1920s a local group of folk singers composed a ditty entitled the *Sidlesham Snail*. The Station Master at Chichester was so annoyed about this tune that he said he would sack any staff member that he heard whistling or singing it.

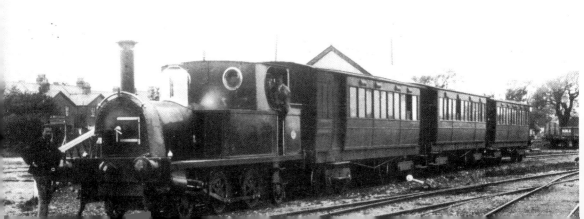

Above:
Manning Wardle saddle tank *Sidlesham*, built in 1861, crosses the canal bridge in 1900 with a train for Selsey, consisting of two Falcon carriages built new for the line in 1896. The bridge mechanism and lifting equipment are clearly seen. *E. C. Griffith collection*

Below left:
What a splendidly unusual locomotive—an outside cylinder 2-4-2T with a sparkling brass dome. This engine *Selsey* was Peckett works No 681 of 1897 and the train of Falcon bogie stock is seen at Selsey in 1900. Later, around 1899 the locomotive was rebuilt extensively with larger tanks and modified coal bunker. It was withdrawn for scrap when the tramway closed in 1935 and cut up in 1936. *Lens of Sutton*

Below:
Jacking and packing the second *Chichester* after a minor accident near Chalder in the late 1920s. In this case the platelayer responsible was found to be at fault for not doing his job properly and was duly dismissed. The locomotive depicted originally belonged to the East Cornwall Mineral Railway, a 3ft 6in gauge mineral line, part of which was taken over by the PD&SWJR in 1908. The locomotive was converted from narrow to standard gauge for use as a shunting locomotive at Callington. It was sold from the PD&SWJR in 1919 and withdrawn in 1932. *E. C. Griffith collection*

Locomotives *Sidlesham* and *Chichester* at Selsey shed in 1898. *Chichester*, a former contractor's locomotive, was extensively rebuilt, and in this photograph is seen painted black, while *Sidlesham* is painted in an ornate lined green livery. *Chichester* was built as an 0-6-0ST by the Long Bottom Railway Foundry in 1847 for the GWR. Later the locomotive was sold to Peckett of Bristol, and in turn it came to the Selsey tramway in 1897.

E. C. Griffith collection

Manning Wardle saddle tank *Morous* in Selsey shed in the late 1920s, showing extensive repairs in progress. *Morous* was originally a contractor's locomotive and worked for the Stratford-on-Avon & Midland Junction Railway before going to the Shropshire & Montgomery-shire Railway in 1910. It was later transferred to the Selsey tramway in 1924 after a number of years out of use and was cut up on site at Chichester in 1936.

Ken Nunn LCGB

The great flood of 1910: *Sidlesham* and ex-GER open wagons are here seen at Sidlesham during the local disaster while repairs were in hand. Train services ceased and a horse bus operated the service.

E. C. Griffith

Above:
Chalder Station in 1900, only a few years after the tramway opened. The buildings along the line were of very similar construction to each other; the station building is built of corrugated iron with its awning having v-shaped upper supports; the platform was faced in concrete and Midland fencing was used. The station nameboard has contractor's lettering style.
E. C. Griffith collection

Top:
A Ford railbus set at Chichester in 1927, showing the station buildings and gas holders in background. The site is now still used to store oil tank wagons from the Southern Region. *Lens of Sutton*

Below:
Derelict coaches of the West Sussex Railway standing at Selsey after closure in 1935. *C. R. L. Coles*

5 THE SHROPSHIRE & MONTGOMERYSHIRE RAILWAY

The story of the Shropshire & Montgomeryshire Railway was long and complicated. It started life in 1866 as the Potteries, Shrewsbury and North Wales Railway. 'The Potts', as it was locally called, was not a great success and through financial troubles the line closed to traffic in 1880. The original company had constructed only the middle section of the line from Shrewsbury to Blodwell Junction, near Nantmawr Quarry. There were a number of moves to reopen the line made locally in the years after the first closure. Several schemes were put forward over the first 20 years of closure, the most notable of which was the Shropshire Railway Company, which was

formed partly by the Potteries shareholders, in a last ditch attempt to retrieve some of their lost money.

The Shropshire Railway Company, formed in the early 1890s, went about raising money to rebuild and reopen the line, but it, like so many schemes of its kind, fell by the wayside and the railway was left to slumber on again until the early years of the 20th century, when the Colonel and the Light Railways Act were to change the situation.

During the period of closure from 1880 until 1910 when the line reopened as the Shropshire and Montgomeryshire Railway, a Mr Reeves looked after the line on behalf of the receiver.

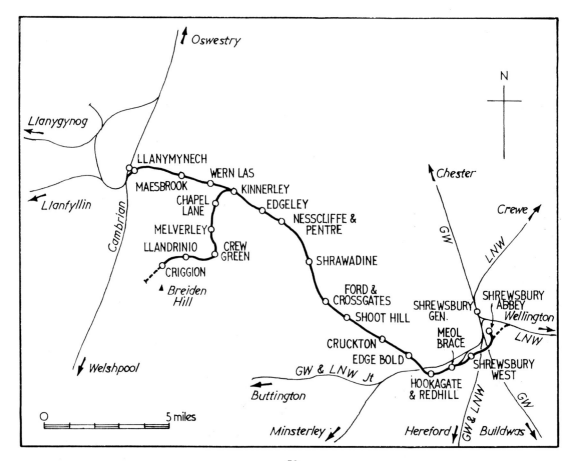

Shrewsbury Abbey Station in about 1870, during the regime of the Potteries, Shrewsbury & North Wales Railway, with an LNWR 0-4-2 and four-wheeled stock.
L&GRP

Mr Reeves had been the guard on the last train of the old Potts and was among the people who travelled on the first train in 1910, when his words to Colonel Stephens were 'now I can die a happy man'.

Guard Reeves patrolled the line with the aid of a plate-layers pump trolley, making sure the fences and permanent way stayed in reasonable order. The receiver had kept a skeleton staff at Shrewsbury and Llanymynech to look after the locomotives and rolling stock, most of which was sold in an auction held at Shrewsbury Abbey Foregate in 1888. The rolling stock which remained, mostly wagons, were left to rot at various locations up and down the line.

During the mid-1900s there was a revival of interest in the campaign to reopen the line, but this time the voices of the local people did not fall on deaf ears, for other people outside the district including the Colonel were also interested. In late 1909 the Colonel had the railway surveyed and new plans were drawn up to reopen it as a light railway. During 1910 contractors moved in and transformed the railway, entangled with weeds and shrubs, with newly relaid track and newly rebuilt buildings; however many of the original buildings built by the old Potteries Railway were renovated and reused for the purpose for which they were built.

During the rebuilding many of the original track components, particularly cast chairs and rails, were torn from their rotten sleepers and used again.

The railway was reopened to traffic on 13 April 1911 amid much public rejoicing in villages along the route of the line, as *Hesperus*, the former LSWR 'Ilfracombe goods' and its train of ex-Midland non-corridor stock, rolled along the line from Shrewsbury Abbey Station to Llanymynech.

The locomotives and rolling stock were maintained at a new shed and workshop built at Kinnerley at the junction of the branch to Criggion; these buildings were adequate not only for light repairs but also for the heaviest of the overhauls required to keep locomotives and stock running on the line. The branch to Criggion was reopened to traffic a year after the main line, in the summer of 1912. It served a quarry at Criggion which was worked by the BQC quarry company.

Although the railway had been easy enough to renovate and reopen, there had been some snags when it came to bridges and the two viaducts along the line. At Shrawardine, on the main line, the structure had to be strengthened and replated, but the wooden trestle at Melverley needed complete rebuilding, the original having collapsed in 1902.

Not all of the former Potteries line was reopened by the Colonel; the Cambrian had purchased the section of line from Llanymynech to Blodwell Junction in 1912 in connection with its Tanat Valley project.

The Colonel purchased a strange variety of stock for the S&M. Locomotive No 1 was the famous diminutive well tank *Gazelle* built by Dodman of Kings Lynn in 1893 for the Mayor of the town. The machine was originally a 2-2-2WT but after its arrival on the Shropshire & Montgomeryshire it was rebuilt as an 0-4-2WT, in order to work with the converted ex-LCC tramcar on the Criggion branch.

As on other lines operated by the Colonel, he also purchased some new locomotives, in this case two 0-6-2Ts from Hawthorn Leslie of Newcastle. The machines were named *Pyramus*, works No 2878 of 1911 and *Thisbe*, works No 2879 also of 1911. After a short time both locomotives were resold to the military authorities, who after the first world war disposed of *Pyramus* to a colliery while retaining *Thisbe* until the late 1930s for use on the Longmoor Military Railway.

Being concerned to provide more motive power than really needed the Colonel overstocked the locomotive shed, in this case with three Terriers, two LSWR 'Ilfracombe goods' 0-6-0s and lastly the most incredible locomotive of all excluding *Gazelle*, a former Bury 0-4-0 originally built for the Shrewsbury & Hereford Railway in 1840. Later rebuilt as an 0-4-2ST, after sale to the Griff Colliery Company in the 1860s, the engine, originally named *Hecate*, and later renamed *Severn*, arrived on the line in 1911 and despite its great age operated trains until the late 1920s.

When most of the steam fleet needed renewal in the late 1920s the Company purchased three LNWR 0-6-0 tender locomotives. The railway had a three-car Ford railbus set and a Ford lorry, which was often coupled to a Ford trailer when working the line.

The Wolseley Sidley car which was used on the Selsey line was stored at Kinnerley for many years, but following its accident on the Selsey line, the machine was never run on the S&M. Austen presumably sent it to Kinnerley from Selsey to use the body for conversion on to the LCC tramcar chassis actually carried out in the late 1930s. The railway lost its passenger service on 6 November 1933; however, parties could still hire a train if they wished and there are many stories of *Gazelle* and its newly refurbished trailer car being used to take people on excursions up the line long after regular passenger trains had gone.

The passenger stock in its day had consisted of a set of four bogie Midland vehicles, several four-wheeled carriages of Midland, North Staffordshire and London & South Western origin, plus one odd Great Eastern vehicle.

An ex-LNWR 0-6-0 heads a train on an outward journey from Llanymynech to Kinnerley in 1931. The train consists of the ex-LSWR royal saloon of 1844 and two ex-Midland bogie non-corridor third class vehicles. Three former LNWR 0-6-0s were purchased for the S&M, LMS Nos 8108, 8182, 8236. In 1939 No 8108 was repainted in Southern Railway olive green and lined. After the War Department took over, the locomotive reverted to black and was given back its old number.
Lens of Sutton

Like the K&ESR, the S&M also had an LSWR Royal carriage of the 1840s, which was later taken to Longmoor. This was used by the Colonel during his yearly inspection of the line.

The goods stock consisted of a variety of Midland, LSWR and NSR wagons. The line carried on through the bad years of the mid-1930s until the outbreak of war in September 1939 when it came under military control. Commercial traffic until then was still being managed from Tonbridge. However, before 1939, Austen had cleared all the derelict rolling stock from Kinnerley yard, which made the line look quite uncommonly neat and tidy.

Shortly after the outbreak of war in 1939, the Army took over and used a number of stations along the route as supply dumps, and continued to do so until 1960 when the line was closed. However, the Criggion branch was not taken over, and trains of stone from the BQC Quarry had to be specially arranged in the Army timetable. For this reason the line had a civilian line controller from the end of the second world war until 1960.

During the years of military operation, the line saw several new types of locomotives and stock, including Austerity 0-6-0STs and GWR Dean goods locomotives, and a set of former LT&SR bogie carriages which were used on the railway to transport Army Staff from one supply dump to the next. These particular coaches were notable since they had corridors and had been built for the Ealing-Southend through service. The final closure came on 29 February 1960, when the last train ran from Llanymynech to Shrewsbury Abbey Station, after which the Army handed over the line to the Western Region for demolition.

Approaching Kinnerley from Llanymynech in 1930 is a double-header consisting of *Pyramus*, an ex-LSWR 'Ilfracombe Goods' 0-6-0, and *Dido* an ex-LBSCR Terrier. The stock again includes Midland four-wheeled full brake and two four-wheel former LSWR coaches. The S&M had three former Brighton A1 Terrier 0-6-0Ts, named *Dido*, *Daphne* and *Hecate*. Unlike other lines run by the Colonel, the Terriers on the S&M were not a great success; this is one of the few photographs showing a Terrier at work on this line.

Real Photographs

Passengers waiting at Shrewsbury Abbey Station in the late 1920s with an LNWR DX 0-6-0 on loan from Shrewsbury LMS shed and a train of ex-Midland stock. In the background are the two water towers that then served the station. The platform water tower is now in the hands of the Tenterden Railway Co, which has taken over part of the Kent & East Sussex as a tourist line, and will be re-erected in the future.

W. H. Austen collection TRC

Kinnerley Junction shed, water tower and approach lines, photographed in September 1938. *L&GRP*

Former LSWR 0-6-0 *Hesperus* at Shrewsbury Abbey Station in late 1937, awaiting the road to Kinnerley with the morning parcels train. Dirty, rusty and leaking steam like a sieve, in this condition the old South Western engine ran for another three years until finally withdrawn under Army control in 1940. *Lens of Sutton*

Kinnerley locomotive shed in the late 1920s showing an 'Ilfracombe goods' 0-6-0 under repair and 0-4-2ST No 2 *Severn* in store. *Severn* had an interesting history; it started life as an 0-4-0 in 1840 on the Shrewsbury & Hereford Railway. Later it was purchased by the Griff Colliery Co and rebuilt as an 0-4-2T in 1911, when it was bought by the Colonel and renamed *Hecate*. Later it reverted to the name *Severn* and was withdrawn in the early 1930s. Note the belt machinery on the far left used for repairing locomotives and stock.

W. H. Austen collection TRC

Gazelle and the Wolseley Sidley trailer at Criggion in 1939 with a Birmingham Locomotive Club special. By this time the locomotive had acquired a coat of Southern olive green with white lining. The locomotive and saloon were used for inspection work, although it was possible to hire both for excursions up the line on weekends. Later during the second world war the locomotive was detached from the saloon and ran as a track testing unit, to sniff out obstacles and mines that might have been laid during the night. After the war both *Gazelle* and the old LSWR royal saloon were sent to Longmoor in Hampshire where it was hoped to preserve them. However the royal saloon was so full of woodworm that it was broken up and burnt. *Gazelle* happily survived to be put at first on a length of track at Longmoor army camp and more recently was sent to York Railway Museum where it can be seen in Longmoor blue livery.   *Lens of Sutton*

Kinnerley locomotive shed in 1911, shortly after completion, showing the Dodman 2-2-2WT *Gazelle* just delivered from T. W. Ward of Sheffield. The locomotive was originally the property of the Mayor of Kings Lynn who was a locomotive enthusiast of the last century. Built by Dodman of Kings Lynn in 1893 to a private order she once journeyed from Kings Lynn to York over the GER and GNR lines. Later after the death of her owner she was sold to T. W. Ward of Sheffield, from whom the Colonel purchased her in 1910 for use as an inspection locomotive.   *LPC Ian Allan*

A very derelict-looking 0-4-2 *Gazelle* in 1935. Fortunately it survived and has been preserved at the National Railway Museum, York.   *L&GRP*

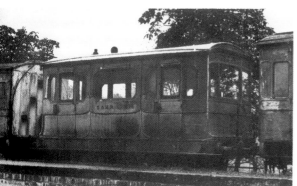

Above:
One of the Midland Railway bogie coaches bought by the Shropshire & Montgomeryshire Railway, seen here soon after arrival. *L&GRP*

Left upper:
One of the pair of former LSW Royal saloons of the 1840s which Colonel Stephens used on two of his lines; this is the one on the Shropshire & Montgomeryshire Railway seen after withdrawal and should be compared with the companion vehicle on the Kent & East Sussex, illustrated on page 26. The S&M vehicle eventually found its way to the Longmoor Military Railway where it was hoped to restore it for preservation but it was found that the bodywork had rotted too badly or been eaten away. *L&GRP*

Left lower:
The former LCC horse tram carriage, here seen dumped at Kinnerley yard in 1935. *Gazelle* was rebuilt from a 2-2-2WT to an 0-4-2WT shortly after its arrival in 1911. The tramcar and the locomotive were paired up to form a makeshift auto-train to operate the Criggion branch passenger service. Later after the closure of the line to passenger traffic the body of the wooden tramcar was removed and replaced with the body of the Wolseley Sidley railcar which had by that time arrived from the Selsey tramway. *Lens of Sutton*

Below:
Kinnerley Junction Station, with a line of passenger coaches photographed in September 1938, five years after passenger services were withdrawn. Nearest the camera are two of the former Midland bogie coaches and fourth from the near end is the former LSWR Royal saloon. *L&GRP*

Shrawardine Station on the Shropshire & Montgomery-shire Railway, with its raised platform and neat timber building. Note the diamond-shaped signal on the platform, face-on to the driver when at danger and edge-on when clear. *L&GRP*

Llanymynech Station showing the western end of the S&M coming in from the left to join the Cambrian line from Oswestry to Welshpool. *L&GRP*

6 THE WESTON, CLEVEDON & PORTISHEAD RAILWAY

The story of the Weston, Clevedon & Portishead Railway is also complex. The line had first been promoted as a tramway to connect the towns of Weston-super-Mare, Clevedon and Portishead. All three north Somerset coastal towns were reached by branches from the Great Western Bristol-Taunton main line but lacked a reliable means of transport to link them together.

After a number of years of dispute and political wrangling, a tramway company was formed in August 1885, to build a tramway to connect the towns. However, financial trouble that had dogged the project for many years reared its ugly head yet again and prolonged matters so much that the line was not started until the late 1880s or early 1890s.

Most of the tramway was to be built through streets or by roadsides, and in some cases ran through fields. The first stage from Weston to Clevedon opened on 1 December 1897, the Company at this time being known as the Weston-super-Mare, Clevedon & Portishead Tramway. A road tramway was constructed from the tram station in Weston and up the main street to the boulevard; because of local protests, it was never opened to traffic, and several more years elasped before the tramway reached Portishead, again following local protests.

In the early days the old company hired its locomotives and managed to purchase a set of American-style carriages built for a railway in South America by the Lancaster Railway Carriage & Wagon Company. The deal for which the carriages were built fell through so the builders were only too pleased to find a customer at home willing to purchase them. Eventually the tramway Company purchased two former Furness Railway 2-2-2WT locomotives, which operated the line for the first decade or so. The railway also carried light goods and parcels traffic which later led to the building of a quay at Wick St Lawrence.

The tramway was at last opened through to Portishead on 7 August 1907, the Company having changed its name to the Weston, Clevedon & Portishead Light Railway in 1899. There were few changes on the line for the first few years after completion in 1907, but in 1911 G. S. Newton resigned as general manager and emigrated to Canada. His place was taken by Colonel Stephens and it is from then that changes began.

Like most of the Colonel's lines, the WC&PR was over-stocked with locomotives. Several WC&PR locomotives were ex-contractors' 0-6-0STs but the line also had its oddities, for example 2-4-0T *Clevedon*, formerly *General Don* of the Jersey Railway and 0-6-0T *Portishead*, later sold to the Renishaw Iron Works.

A former Furness Railway 2-2-2WT built in 1857 and sold to the WC&PR in 1904 here seen crossing the Yeo Bridge in 1898 with a train of Lancaster Carriage and Wagon Co American bogie vehicles bound for Weston. The six American bogie vehicles were originally built for South America but the order was cancelled and the WC&PR purchased the vehicles at a reduced price.
LPC Ian Allan

A railway-owned horse bus at Weston in the 1900s. The Company at this time operated a horse bus between its station and the pier. Later the service ceased when local transport improved. *W. H. Austen collection TRC*

A notable machine was the Sharp Stewart 2-4-0T *Hesperus*, formerly owned by the Princes Risborough & Watlington Railway and latterly by the Great Western. Because of its name the locomotive was jokingly called 'The Wreck' by the shed staff.

Towards the end of the 1930s the Company purchased two Brighton A1X Terrier tank locomotives from the Southern Railway. They were later taken over by the Great Western which overhauled them, but could find little work for them. The last to survive, WC&PR No 2 *Portishead* was cut up in 1954 at Swindon.

For a time at the end of the first world war Kent & East Sussex Railway *Northiam* ran on the line but was sent home early in 1920. The line also had two railcars, but unlike the rather crude Ford and Shefflex railbuses used on the other lines managed by the Colonel, the WC&PR vehicles were quite sophisticated. The Company had a Drewry four-wheeled railcar and trailer which it purchased new in 1922, and a large Drewry car purchased secondhand from the Southern Railway, which had previously experimented with it on the Lydd branch in Kent.

The Colonel also purchased two Muir Hill tractors for shunting the Wick St Lawrence branch; the first, which resembled a farm tractor on rail wheels, was damaged beyond repair in an accident while being towed in 1925. The second, which looked like a garden shed on wheels, was delivered in 1926 and worked satisfactorily until the line closed in 1940.

The railway's carriage stock was fascinating for in addition to the set of American bogie carriages the line had several Metropolitan four-wheeled vehicles and some LSWR four-wheeled carriages; the Company also had a Great Eastern four-wheeled brake van. It was common at one time to run the small Drewry and a Metropolitan four-wheeled carriage coupled together. However this practice ceased when the Drewry's trailer arrived. The goods vehicles consisted of Midland and Great Eastern vehicles which were only used for the line's internal traffic.

The buildings were quite substantial wooden

and brick structures at main stations. At halts small neat wooden shelters were built. The locomotive depot and workshop was situated at Clevedon, although rolling stock was sometimes repaired at Portishead.

The railway mostly served the tourists in the area although, in the off-peak season, local goods and farm produce predominated. The line held its own through the 1920s and early 1930s but by 1936 the railway began to feel the pinch from the motor bus operators and the depression. The Colonel had operated a small fleet of coastal craft in the 1920s and most of this fleet, which transported goods from the South Wales coast to Wick St Lawrence Quay, was sold by the mid-1930s leaving a gap in the railway's economy.

The Colonel tried several experiments in an attempt to ease the cost of running and maintaining the line. One idea involved using individual concrete slabs under each rail instead of wooden sleepers. The slabs were held together by old point and signal rodding. The same thing was also tried on part of the Kent & East Sussex railway in early 1930s, near Headcorn. It was one of the first applications of concrete as sleepers, today used in many parts of the world.

After the Colonel died the line passed into the hands of Austen, who was appointed receiver by the shareholders. Austen managed the line through the last difficult years until the outbreak of war in September 1939 but it was at this time that the Excess Insurance Company bought out all the other shareholders and gave Austen orders to close the line from 18 May 1940. Economic circumstances finally won.

Despite the war a large number of people turned out to see the last train run between Portishead and Weston-super-Mare. However, all was not quite over because, following the invasion of France by the Germans, the South Wales ports were jammed full of coal normally exported to the French ports. The Government ordered the Great Western to take over the WC&PR together with any serviceable rolling stock and to use the railway for coal storage. The only stock worth having as far as the GWR was concerned were the two Brighton A1X Terriers No 2 *Portishead* and No 4.

After overhaul the locomotives were operated by the GWR first on the WC&PR and then at locations on the GWR, but were found to be lacking power for heavy work. They became GWR Nos 5 and 6; the latter was cut up in 1948 but No 5 survived until 1954. The rest of the rolling stock was sold and cut up in late 1940 or early 1941. WC&P saddle tank No 5, built in 1919 by Manning Wardle, was sold out of service to industry in late 1940.

The Great Western abandoned the temporary use of the line in mid-1941 and the scrap merchants moved in; by mid-1942 the railway had been lifted. Much of the old rail had originally come from the Krupp Steel Works of Essen and now it was destined to return there in a very different shape.

Today little survives of the line. Most of the buildings are no more and the track bed has largely been obliterated by building and reclamation by farmers.

Manning Wardle 0-6-0ST No 5, at Clevedon with a train
of former Metropolitan four-wheelers ready to leave for
Weston in 1923. This locomotive was acquired in 1919
in practically new condition. In its early days it bore the
name *Hecate*. Later, before 1923, these plates were
removed and it ran from then until 1940, when it was
sold for industrial use, without a name. The carriages are
Metropolitan. Note the Midland open wagon next to
rear carriage, probably then only recently purchased for
the line's internal traffic when this photograph was
taken.   *Ken Nunn LCGB*

Right:
One of the former LBSCR Terrier 0-6-0Ts, originally No
53 *Ashtead*, built in 1875, and sold to the Weston,
Clevedon & Portishead becoming No. 4. It became
GWR property in 1940 and bore the number 6 but was
scrapped in 1948.   *L&GRP*

A scene at Clevedon locomotive shed in 1929 showing
former Jersey Railway 2-4-0T *General Don,* renamed
Clevedon, No 1 on the WC&PR. Behind is seen ex-GWR
2-4-0T No 1384 and WC&PR No 4 *Hesperus*. *Clevedon*
was not well liked by the locomotive crews.
                                          Author's collection

The former GWR 2-4-0T No 1384 seen here at Weston
in 1911, shortly after its acquisition. This locomotive had
a very interesting background. It was built by Sharp
Stewart in 1876 and first worked on the Princes
Risborough & Watlington Railway, which was later
acquired by the GWR. After this it became No 1384,
spending most of the rest of her GWR career on various
short branch lines on that company's system. In 1911 it
was acquired by the WC&PR for use on passenger
trains. It was withdrawn in mid-1930s and cut up in
1940, after the line's closure.   *LPC Ian Allan*

Above:
A general view of Clevedon Station shed and works taken in June 1937.   L&GRP

Left:
Roadside halt at Broadstone consisting of nothing more than a level crossing and a hut.   L&GRP

Below:
The small Drewry petrol railcar of 1921, here seen at Portishead in the early 1920s. Summer passenger traffic, particularly at weekends, could be heavy at this time. The small Drewry had an unpowered trailer which was also often used with the large Drewry car. Unlike the Ford and Shefflex sets on the other lines managed by the Colonel, the Drewry cars were quite advanced in their design and were much more comfortable to travel in.   *Photomatic/H. Smith collection*

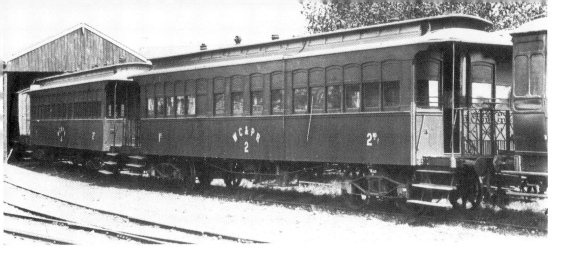

Above:
Two of the WC&P's end balcony bogie coaches purchased from the Lancaster Railway Carriage & Wagon Co after a cancelled South American order.
L&GRP

Among the WC&P's rolling stock were some old four-wheel coaches bought secondhand from other railways; *below* is a pair of LSW close-coupled four-wheel saloons and *bottom* a pair of former Metropolitan third class coaches. Notice the additional lower footboards provided to give access from low level platforms.
L&GRP

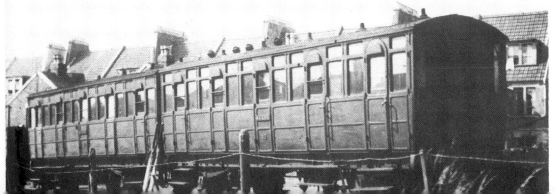

The WC&P was nothing if not modern when it came to control of level crossings, at least where it passed over the main Bristol-Weston road. Traffic lights were installed to control road traffic, triggered off when the train operated a treadle at the approaches to the crossing. (*Left*). Traffic light indications were also displayed to the approaching train with a green aspect shown when the lights for road traffic were at red.

L&GRP

Below:
Wick St Lawrence wharf near the mouth of the River Yeo, used for transferring goods from the small coastal fleet, also owned by Colonel Stephens, which plied between South Wales ports and Wick St Lawrence.

L&GRP

7 THE ASHOVER LIGHT RAILWAY

The Ashover Light Railway was the last narrow gauge line to be built by the Colonel. The line served a group of stone quarries owned by the Clay Cross Company in Derbyshire. It ran from Clay Cross on the LMS main line between Derby and Chesterfield to Ashover Butts. Along its course it served a number of stone quarries and an open-cast coal mine, near Chesterfield Road Station. The mainstay of the traffic was granite chippings used by the LMS for ballast and for which the Company had a permanent contract.

The idea of a light railway connecting the quarries was first put forward by the Clay Cross Company before the first world war, but indecision and the outbreak of war prevented anything being done until 1919 when the

Jackson family, the owners of the Clay Cross Company, rekindled interest in the scheme.

It was intended from the start that the line would be a mineral line, and no thought was given to operating a passenger service; however, the Board of Trade had other intentions and the Company was slowly coaxed into the idea of a passenger service, much to the annoyance of the Jackson family.

Originally the line was to be standard gauge, but with material shortages after the war and on the advice given by Colonel Stephens, the Clay Cross management agreed to a 60cm gauge line instead, since narrow gauge materials were available having been used to provide supply railways in Europe during the conflict. The first

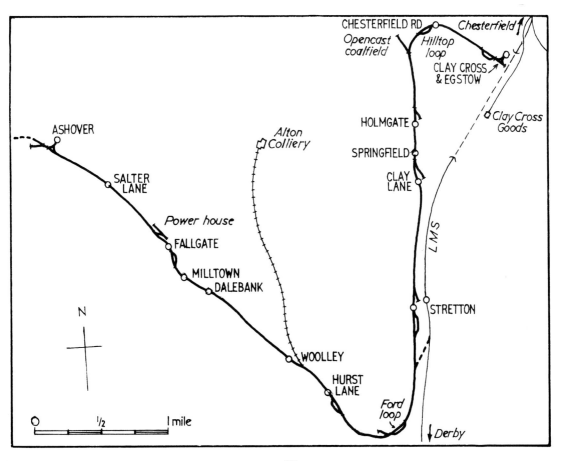

67

sod was cut at Fallgate on 22 December 1922 and work steadily progressed over the next two years until spring 1924 when a special train worked through from Clay Cross to Fallgate, invited guests riding in open wagons for the occasion. T. H. Jackson rode in fine style seated in his armchair.

Originally the Company purchased four Baldwin 4-6-0Ts from the War Disposals Board. These locomotives had been used by the British Army on the western front ordnance light railways of the war, together with a fleet of Hudson bogie open wagons for stone traffic. The locomotives were named after the children of General Jackson, the acting General Manager of the Clay Cross Company. Of the first four the names were *Guy*, *Hummy*, *Peggy* and *Joan*; later two more locomotives were purchased from T. W. Ward of Sheffield, also Baldwin 4-6-0Ts, one being named *Bridget* and the second being given *Guy*'s nameplates when it was found that the original locomotive bearing that name was in need of extensive repairs.

The original *Guy* was later stored at Clay Cross carriage shed until dismantled for spare parts between 1939 and 1942, when the remains were cut up for scrap.

The passenger carriages used on the railway were built by the Gloucester Railway Carriage & Wagon Company in 1924, and were numbered 1 to 4 on the Company's list. Each vehicle was vacuum braked and had a centre coupling. The carriage bodies were new, but the running gear was second hand WD Hudson bogies purchased from the War Disposals Board.

The stations along the line were built shortly after the railway had opened to mineral traffic. The buildings were quite unlike any of the buildings on the other railways operated by the Colonel. All were of wood, some having a combined office and goods store, and others having just a simple but neat shelter. At Ashover Butts a cafe was built, and named *Where the Rainbow Ends*; it was here that the staff would often while away the time between turns on the passenger service.

The railway formally opened to passenger traffic on the 6 April 1925. T. H. Jackson at the age of 91 officiated at the ceremony and travelled on the first train. Although the day went well, and for some time the little railway was very popular with the locals, the management was still not happy at having to run passenger trains.

Ashover Butts' Station soon after the opening of the line in 1925. The station was located just outside the village at the bottom of a hill. The run round facilities here were in the form of a triangle, where the complete train reversed and then backed into the platform after turning. Note the building with its office on one side and goods store on the other, also in the foreground the former WD bogie open wagons lettered ALR. Like most of the stock they were purchased secondhand as war surplus by the company. *LPC Ian Allan*

In the late 1920s and early 1930s the railway played its part in transportation for the district. Not only were ordinary everyday trains run but also special Sunday and Bank Holiday excursions. Nevertheless when the passenger service started to make a loss in 1930 the management of the Clay Cross Company wasted no time in suggesting that all passenger services should be terminated and from the end of October 1931 the line ceased to operate regular passenger trains.

However, passenger trains still operated during the summer and on bank holidays until September 1936, when the carriages were stored in a siding near Ashover Butts, in case the need arose for their use again. In addition to the original bogie carriages, the Company purchased eight short-wheelbase bogie vehicles from the Wembley Exhibition when it closed in late 1925. These were the carriages which had been in use on the Exhibition's Never-stop railway and were badly needed because of the gross overcrowding owing to the popularity of the Ashover line in its first season. Later after the line closed to passenger traffic, the Never-stop vehicles were shunted into a siding and left to decay, finally being broken up in 1942. The Company also purchased one of the former Leek & Manifold transporter wagons to carry standard gauge wagons, which was not a great success after its gauge was altered from 2ft 6in to 60cm. This vehicle was broken up with other items of rolling stock in 1942.

The railway enjoyed a new lease of life during the second world war when the quarries and open-cast coal mine were very active. Often at this time a Baldwin would haul a train of full

Baldwin 4-6-0T *Peggy* and train near Chesterfield Road shortly after opening of the ALR in 1925. The locomotives and carriage stock were elaborately lined during this period, the livery being Midland Crimson Lake lined in yellow straw. The goods stock was painted in light grey with white lettering shaded black. Note the stove-pipe chimney with its rainwater flap on the Baldwin. Later the stove pipes were replaced with chimneys of a heavier cast type. *LPC Ian Allan*

stone wagons from Ashover to Chesterfield Road where it would pick up a further load of coal and continue to Clay Cross, with the stone wagons behind and the coal wagons coupled in front. During the latter part of the war the Baldwins started to wear out, and gradually one by one the locomotives were cannibalised to provide parts to keep sister machines in traffic.

The Company had purchased ten 60cm gauge Dick, Kerr petrol-electric locomotives shortly after the first world war. These machines were not used as locomotives but were used as stationary generators for a number of years.

One of the petrol locomotives, later named *Amos*, was overhauled at the Company's works at Clay Cross in 1928 and set to work shunting the yard at Clay Cross and banking stone trains up the incline at Hurst Lane. It was later rebuilt and re-gauged to run on standard gauge track. *Amos* was scrapped in 1964 after being sold out of service to a contractor.

A Muir Hill geared tractor was purchased in 1940 for use in Fallgate Yard but was rarely used; it resembled a Fordson tractor on a narrow gauge frame and was cut up in 1945. The Muir Hill was replaced by a Planet diesel locomotive which shunted Fallgate Yard for a time before being sold to George Cohen, for use on one of his contracts on Canvey Island. This was replaced with a Ransome-Rapier diesel unit which was used until the system closed completely in 1963.

After the war the stone traffic began to decline and in 1948 when the railways were nationalised the Clay Cross Company lost the contract for ballast. The railway slowly closed down between 1948 and 1950 when the line was abandoned completely although the yard at Fallgate carried on functioning, using diesel locomotives, until late 1963. All repairs to locomotives and rolling stock were carried out at the Company's workshops at Clay Cross and it was here that the remaining Baldwins and some of the open wagons were cut up in 1951.

Today little remains of the railway. The Planet diesel has been privately preserved and a number of small relics from the line are in private hands. These include some of the nameplates on display at the narrow-gauge museum at Towyn. Also two of the carriages are preserved on the Lincolnshire Coast Light Railway. *Where the Rainbow Ends* cafe was re-erected at Clay Cross Sports Ground and is still there.

In the years after the passenger service had ceased special passenger trains were still worked using open wagons fitted with seats. These trains were run for the Clay Cross Company workers on Bank Holidays and company sports days when trains were run between Clay Cross and Ashover Butts. The train is seen here at Ashover Butts during a bank holiday in 1946 with Baldwin 4-6-0T *Joan* in charge.   *Real Photographs*

An unidentified Baldwin 4-6-0T at Woolley in the heart of rural Derbyshire in 1946 with a train of stone, bound for Clay Cross LMS exchange sidings. In the latter years of the line most of the traffic from the stone quarries was for the LMS for use as permanent way ballast. This traffic ceased at nationalisation in 1948. The cancellation of this regular traffic was a major factor in the decision by the Clay Cross Company to close the line.   *I. Gotheridge collection*

A battered *Peggy* takes water at Clay Cross stone crushing plant in 1949, with a stone train for the exchange sidings. There were only two serviceable Baldwins at this time, *Peggy* and *Joan*. Although *Peggy* was the locomotive in regular use (*Joan* being an unpopular locomotive because it was rough riding), both were cut up on site at Clay Cross in 1951.

H. Skinner collection

A rear end shot of Baldwin 4-6-0T *Peggy* in 1946, showing the cab, rebuilt by Driver H. Skinner using the front spectacle plate of Baldwin locomotive *Guy*. By this time the locomotives were painted unlined black; the locomotive is in a very messy condition with rust and grime everywhere. Note the water hose on the rear bunker for washing down the footplate, and on the rear buffer beam is the nozzle for the vacuum brake, then long since out of use. *H. Skinner collection*

Roll over Baldwin, the second *Guy*, after a tiff with a shale lorry at Clay Cross about 1940. The locomotive was later repaired and put back to work. The unusual shot clearly shows the cylinder blocks and valve gear. *I. Gotheridge collection*

8 THE RYE & CAMBER TRAMWAY

The Rye & Camber Tramway was the Colonel's second line and was opened to traffic in stages between 1895-1908. The first stage opened to traffic on 13 July 1895 and ran from Rye to Golf Links; the second stage opened 13 years later on 13 July 1908 and extended the line from Golf Links to Camber Sands.

The line was only 2½ miles in length and was laid in 25lb flat bottom rail with a gauge of 3ft. For the opening the Company purchased only one locomotive, a Bagnall 2-4-0T, named *Camber*, works No 1461 of 1895. It was joined in 1897 by a second machine, again built by Bagnall of Stafford, 2-4-0T works No 1511 of 1897 named *Victoria*, presumably because it was Jubilee year.

The second locomotive was of larger dimensions with a greater tractive effort. In the early days of the Camber tram, the Colonel had designed an internal combustion engined locomotive, possibly the first of its kind in the world. It was based on the Ackroyd principle, but apart from the drawing stage, the project came to nothing.

The rolling stock used on the line is of interest. For the opening the line had only one carriage, which had been supplied by Bagnall

with the locomotive. It was a 1st/2nd saloon, with doors on one side only; it was later joined by a second vehicle, an all-3rd saloon built locally by the Rother Ironworks in the town of Rye. In addition to the passenger carriages the tramway owned a fleet of four-wheeled open wagons, which were used to collect shingle for ballast from the beach at Camber. The buildings were constructed from corrugated iron with wooden framing. Stations were sited at Rye, Halfway House (Golf Links), and Camber. The locomotive depot, again a corrugated iron affair, was erected at the Rye end of the line.

The Camber tram was very popular with the summer visitors to Rye, and was used a great deal by the golfers in the district. The line was above all a tourist attraction, transporting people from Rye to Camber Sands and giving a joyride to adults and children at the same time.

Several tales of the Camber tram have been handed down including one involving golfers who full of sporting fun, had a habit of pulling out the pin between the first and second carriage, which sometimes resulted in the passengers in the second vehicle being left stranded between Rye and Golf Links Station. After a while the drivers became used to this

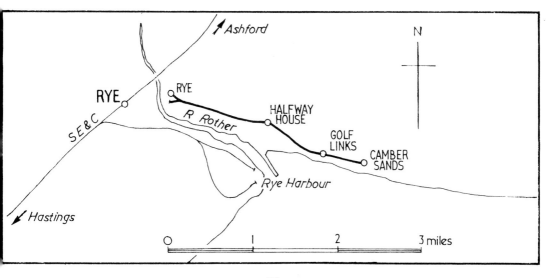

74

prank and quickly returned to pick up the lost vehicle.

The tramway acquired a third locomotive in 1925, a petrol locomotive built by the Kent Construction Company; the machine, though ugly in appearance, proved successful in everyday use, It is believed that the Kent Construction Company were sales representatives for Simplex.

By the late 1930s the line had become so popular that the management decided to extend it again to the site of the new holiday camp then being constructed at Camber Sands. The new extension was just completed when the war broke out in September 1939 and was never opened to traffic.

The line closed at the end of the 1939 season for the duration of the war, during which numerous supply dumps were built in the Rye

area. In order to give easy access to the military lorries the track bed, together with the track was concreted over in several locations. After the war the cost of putting everything in order was too much for the Company and the concern went into voluntary liquidation.

It was planned to take one of the locomotives, *Camber*, to Rolvenden in 1939 for overhaul before the expected opening of the holiday camp extension. This plan was never carried out and both the remaining locomotives (*Camber* and the petrol locomotive) were sold for scrap in 1946 along with the remaining rolling stock.

Victoria, the second locomotive, had previously been sold for scrap in 1932 after the arrival of the petrol locomotive. One of the carriages partially survived scrapping—its underframe and roof are now preserved at the Narrow Gauge Railway Museum at Brockham.

Tram approaching Rye station from Halfway House halt with locomotive *Victoria* at the head and both bogie carriages. The man on the front balcony of the Bagnall carriage is conductor-guard Percy Sheppard. Note the iron boundary fencing.   *Ken Nunn LCGB*

Camber and *Victoria* at Rye in 1921 showing the difference in size between the two locomotives. *Camber* was the first, delivered in 1895; the larger locomotive, *Victoria*, arrived on the line in 1897. Behind it are both carriages and the roof of the tram station. Note the sand covers over the cylinder slide bars of locomotives, and doors on non-platform side of track.   *LPC Ian Allan*

Two four-wheeled sand wagons at Camber in the early 1920s. Note the fabric covers over the grease axleboxes to keep sand out, and the catch over the top, to hold the sides in.   *LCGB Ken Nunn collection*

Golf Links Station was situated on the edge of the sand dunes near Camber where a train headed by 2-4-0T *Camber* is just leaving for Rye.　　*L&GRP*

Golf links station in 1925, showing the building and track layout. The station building is not unlike Hawkhurst station in its outward appearance, being built of corrugated iron and wood; also note the ornate barge boards and lattice wooden fence, rather like the style of fence at Midland stations.　　*Ken Nunn LCGB*

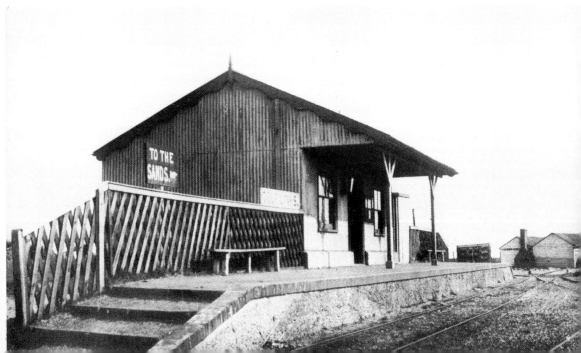

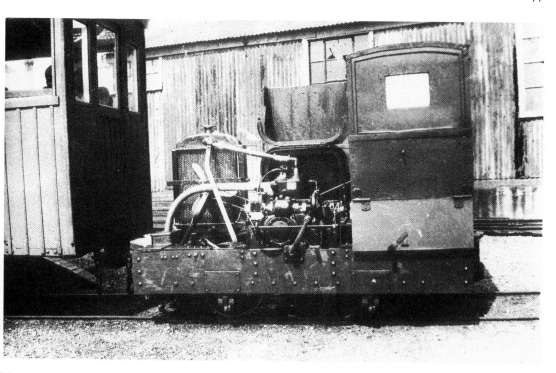

The petrol locomotive supplied by the Kent Construction Co at Rye in 1932 just out of works, showing the petrol engine and cab. Note the end of Bagnall carriage, showing end windows and door.

LPC Ian Allan

The petrol tractor and bogie carriages at Camber sands in 1935, a year or two after the new petrol locomotive went into service. It is seen here painted in unlined light green; the steam locomotives were originally painted light green and lined, but *Victoria* was painted in unlined light green without its name after 1920. Both carriages were painted in dark brown. *Victoria* was withdrawn for scrap in 1933 after the petrol tractor's arrival.

Ken Nunn LCGB

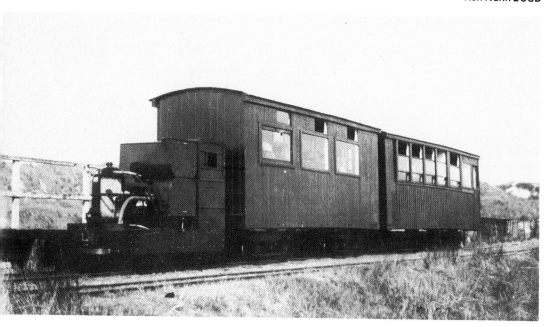

9 THE FESTINIOG RAILWAY (For Welsh Highland Railway—see page 82)

The Festiniog Railway is one of the most famous narrow gauge railways in the world. Many articles and books have been written about this historic line but Colonel Stephens' connections date only from 1923, when he took over the locomotive superintendency and civil engineer's positions of both the Festiniog and Welsh Highland railways until his death in 1931, after which Austen and his team looked after both railways until they closed.

The Festiniog was opened as a horse tramway on 20 April 1836. It was built to the 60cm gauge and ran from Porthmadog to Blaenau Ffestiniog, where it served the local slate quarries. In 1863

the railway made history by being the first narrow-gauge line to use steam locomotives. Much of this great achievement can be put down to the Spooner family who not only engineered the Festiniog but were also responsible for the setting up of the ill-fated North Wales Narrow Gauge Railway. The story of the FR as a Stephens line really begins after the first world war. The Festiniog had enjoyed great prosperity in pre-war days, but such times did not return after the conflict was over and because of a combination of the slump in the slate industry and road competition, the company's receipts looked pretty grim in the early 1920s.

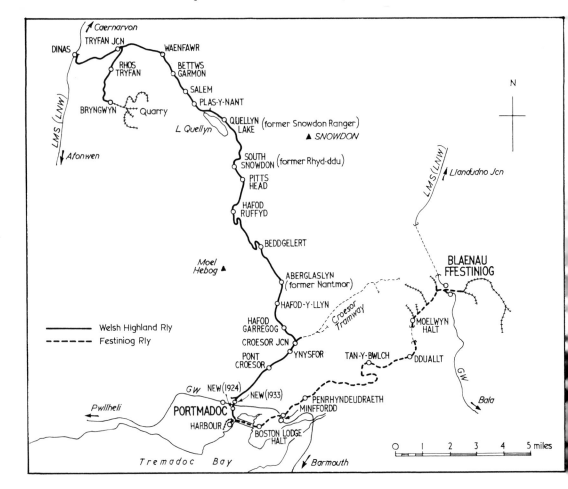

The Colonel by this time had earned himself a reputation for his ability to run unremunerative light railways, which prompted the Board of the Festiniog Railway to ask him to join the Company in a managerial capacity, in order to try and put the books straight.

It so happened that the Colonel was engaged with the Welsh Highland Light Railway in a similar position around this time and although the two concerns were run from Tonbridge, they remained independent until 1934 when the Festiniog had to bail out the unfortunate Welsh Highland, after the shareholders threatened to close the line.

At the time of the Colonel's appointment in early 1923 the Festiniog was a very interesting railway, for the Spooner concept of a narrow gauge main line railway still prevailed. Not that Colonel Stephens ever understood this for he waged a continual war on the management and staff of both North Wales lines for most of his latter years.

The locomotives and rolling stock were in good condition, although in some cases in need of overhaul, and the buildings, quite unlike the structures on the Colonel's other lines were constructed of sturdy local stone and slate. In the spirit of a main line the Festiniog was fully signalled with semaphores and disc-and-crossbar types. The permanent way was well kept and regularly relaid, using bullhead rail on cast chairs, unlike most other narrow-gauge lines which generally used flat bottomed rail and dog spikes. At the Blaenau Ffestiniog end of the line the Company had joint facilities with both the GWR and the LMS in addition to several yards connecting the various slate quarries in the district.

The line to Dinas, which had lost its passenger service in 1870, was still thriving with slate traffic. The workshops were at Boston Lodge, and were like a Swindon or Crewe, when compared with Rolvenden or Selsey, and were more than well equipped to handle the most difficult of repairs and overhauls.

All the day-to-day administration was carried out from Harbour Station and it was here that the resident line manager presided over the affairs of the FR Company and also later the Welsh Highland, in addition to his original responsibilities.

The locomotives during this period comprised an interesting mixture of 0-4-0STs rebuilt from the original George England locomotives, and the later development of 0-4-4-0 double Fairlie locomotives—not the sort of motive power common on a narrow-gauge light railway. In addition to this the railway had a fleet of bogie and four-wheel carriages, some of which were used only on quarrymen's trains, whereas the bogie vehicles operated on the through services from Porthmadog to Blaenau Ffestiniog.

The FR had a large fleet of goods vehicles ranging from covered vans and gunpowder vans to wooden open wagons and slate wagons. Most of the slate quarries had private fleets of vehicles, together with the GWR and LMS who had their own narrow-gauge slate wagons.

The Colonel was responsible for the introduction of internal combustion locomotives to the line shortly after his appointment in 1923. They were an armour-plated Simplex tractor, ex-War Department, purchased for use on shunting duties, and a gas-electric 0-4-0 locomotive from the American Army, built to a Baldwin design by the Pittsburgh Model Engineering Company. Both locomotives still operate on the Festiniog today, the Simplex being named *Mary Ann* and the Baldwin, rebuilt to a 2-4-0, is named *Moelwyn*.

The Festiniog suffered badly during the depression of the late 1920s and early 1930s, when road competition took away much of the local goods trade and a number of slate quarries closed down, although the summer tourist traffic still boomed, which helped the Company get over some of the financial problems. The Colonel was very autocratic and would often drop in at the wrong time to see how things were going. On these occasions the staff would quickly put their defensive plans into action. One early warning signal adopted by the locomotive drivers was to stroke their beards as the train carrying the Colonel pulled into each station; in this way the station staff knew he was on the train.

The Colonel always had an annual tour around Boston Lodge Works, during which he had all the working locomotives lined up in a row to inspect them. If he found anything wrong he would fly into a temper and make acid remarks about the defect and order the guilty individual to put it right immediately. On one occasion the Colonel referred to the fact that the locomotive inspection pits at Boston Lodge were so dirty and disgusting that a rat would think twice before jumping in and drowning in them.

The Colonel would sometimes return to

Tonbridge and send a starchy memo outlining his grounds for displeasure. Most of the memos were thrown into the bin by the recipients, which made relations even worse. The Colonel was made Chairman and Managing Director of both the Festiniog and Welsh Highland in 1925. After he died in October 1931 the line passed into the hands of Mr Austen, who along with the Festiniog Board operated services until 16 September 1939 when all passenger trains ceased. The Company meanwhile had taken over the unfortunate Welsh Highland Railway in 1934, a move which helped to bankrupt the Festiniog Railway. The Railway operated a goods train service until late 1946 when all services were suspended. The line was left to nature until 1951 when a preservation society was formed to reopen the line, from Porthmadog to Blaenau Ffestiniog. The Railway now enjoys an ever-increasing summer traffic and slowly but surely over the last quarter century the new company has reopened the line, little by little back towards Blaenau Ffestiniog.

THE FREDERICK HOTELS.
LIMITED.

HOTEL GREAT ... CENTRAL, LONDON
HOTEL RUSSELL, LONDON.—
HOTEL MAJESTIC, HARROGATE
ROYAL PAVILION HOTEL, FOLKESTONE
LORD WARDEN HOTEL, DOVER ■
SACKVILLE HOTEL, BEXHILL-ON-SEA
HOTEL METROPOLE, WHITBY

Lord Warden Hotel,
Dover.

TELEGRAMS: WARDEN, DOVER.
TELEPHONE. DOVER 413.
(PRIVATE BRANCH EXCHANGE.)

12. 6. 1926

Dear W.H.A.,

I think you have done very well. I'm sorry re weather. The people on the F.R. are quite different to our people, as you have found out by now. I found it out long ago. They can't help it, it's their nature. We have got to put up with it whilst we have the job.

Re trucks – what strikes me is the sudden drop. They could not have finished all the "slightly damaged" in one certain week!! Tell them to pick a few light repairs to bring the numbers up. There is some game on probably, a scheme, between them to stop shortening hands as work draws to a close. Re weeds and grass. Can you get this mown to rail level and after it is dry, or partly so, set fire to.

The crossing where the engine came off at Dinas probably has loose V bolts, a lot of them have. Griffiths does not seem to look after them and have them screwed up. Can you look at this and get it done. I want all the old signal quadrants (the things used in place of levers) collected and sent to Boston Lodge for scrap, also broken chairs.

I have told Williams* to put all the shirkers in Boston Lodge on 4 days a week short time starting Monday = 32 hours a week each. The wages bill must be reduced.

Yours faithfully

H. Stephens

P.S. Bad weather here, a big gale yesterday.

One of Colonel Stephens' letters to W. H. Austen regarding work standards on the Festiniog Railway.

Double Fairlie locomotive *Taliesin* and Porthmadog-bound train at Tan-y-Bwlch in the early 1930s. The train is made up of Festiniog bogie carriages and a short wheelbase brake third, next to the locomotive. At this time most of the carriage stock was painted green with black panelling, while locomotives were painted in unlined dark olive green. However, the front brake vehicle is in light brown livery.   *Lens of Sutton*

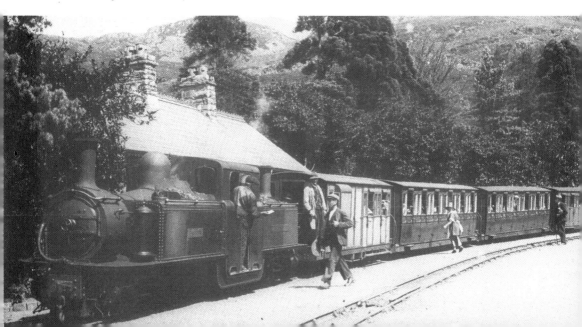

Shunting slates at Blaenau Ffestiniog in 1920, with England saddle tank *Welsh Pony* built in 1867. The ornate green livery with its square panel lining dates from pre first world war days. In the station yard in the background is the LNWR goods shed and behind are the quarry inclines and slate tips.   *Ken Nunn'LCGB*

Armour-plated ex-Light Railway Operations Department Simplex petrol rail tractor at Harbour Station in 1925, showing the controls, hand brake and the petrol tank on the far side of the driver's seat. This petrol tractor is still alive and well, and now named *Mary Ann*.
Real Photographs

A double Fairlie pounds towards Tan-y-Bwlch, through the steeply sided cutting approaching the station, with a train of mixed stock consisting of quarrymen's coaches known as bug boxes, and bogie vehicles.
Real Photographs

10 THE WELSH HIGHLAND RAILWAY (See map on page 78)
(Formerly the North Wales Narrow Gauge Railway)

The Welsh Highland Railway had its origins in the early 1870s when the Spooner family promoted the North Wales Narrow Gauge Railway which ran from Dinas, on the LNWR Afonwen-Caernarvon line, to Rhyd-ddu, later South Snowdon. The NWNGR had a branch which ran from Tryfan Junction to Bryngwyn but this lost its passenger service quite early in the line's history, on 15 August 1877.

The railway opened to traffic on 21 May 1877 and right from the beginning ran at a loss. The only time when any money could be made was when the tourists visited the area in the peak summer months. The Company carried on until just before the outbreak of world war I in August 1914. In December 1913 the passenger service had ceased over the whole line followed by complete closure to traffic of the line on the 31 October 1916. Much of the original rolling stock was sold for further use by military railways.

The line was then left derelict for five years, until, shortly after the war, Colonel Stephens surveyed the railway to ascertain its potential as a light railway. He also planned to extend the line south through Beddgelert and the Aberglaslyn Pass over part of the former Croesor Tramway to Porthmadog where it would join the Festiniog Railway.

Work commenced on the reconstruction of the NWNGR in late 1921 and the first stage of the new Company's line from Dinas to Beddgelert was opened on 31 July 1922. The railway changed its name from the North Wales Narrow Gauge Railway to the Welsh Highland Railway in July 1922. The final extension was commissioned on 1 June 1923, when the line was connected to the Festiniog at Porthmadog.

The Welsh Highland ran across the Cambrian line at Porthmadog and then down the High Street to Harbour Station, the Welsh Highland station being named Porthmadog New Station. The buildings along the new through line were a mixture of stone-built structures, as on the former NWNGR, and primitive corrugated-iron buildings, as at stations south of South Snowdon.

Porthmadog New Station was merely a collection of corrugated-iron buildings to the north of the Cambrian-Welsh Highland level crossing; at one stage the Festiniog and Welsh Highland trains ran from the New Station but this changed in the early 1930s when the FR reverted to Harbour Station.

The Welsh Highland's shed and workshop was situated at Dinas, although often locomotives were sent to Boston Lodge for heavy repairs.

Quite unlike the Festiniog, the Welsh Highland was not a main line narrow-gauge railway, and it is here that the Colonel misunderstood the whole concept of the Spooner principle. The Festiniog, and for that matter the North Wales Narrow Gauge Railway, were built not as light railways but as narrow gauge main lines, fully signalled, with sturdy earthworks and buildings. The Colonel could not grasp that both lines were designed to allow narrow-gauge trains to run at speeds higher than on some standard gauge branches; worse, he was very dogmatic about his way of doing things and even though the men of the Festiniog and WHR knew their jobs and ran their railways extremely well, he always knew better, which caused a great deal of criticism on both lines.

The Welsh Highland inherited two locomotives from the NWNGR, together with some goods rolling stock. Colonel Stephens added to this stock by purchasing an ex-War Department Baldwin 4-6-0T of the same class as the locomotives used on the Ashover and Snailbeach lines. This machine, which bore the number 590, was not a great success on the line and as the locomotive crews and shed staff disliked it intensely, the Baldwin was mostly used on goods trains, while the ex-NWNGR 0-6-4T *Moel Tryfan* and 2-6-2T *Russell* were used on passenger duties.

The original NWNGR coaches with Cleminson radial trucks had been replaced by a fleet of eleven bogie carriages, one of which was rebuilt as a buffet car in 1934. The goods vehicles varied from iron-built slate wagons and

Beddgelert on the Welsh Highland, with Festiniog Railway 0-4-0STT No 5 in the foreground about to leave for Portmadog, and WHR 2-6-2T *Russell* standing with a train from Dinas.

wooden open wagons borrowed from the FR to ex-Croesor Tramway open wagons and NWNGR vans.

Apart from tourism during the summer the line relied heavily on the few quarries in the Moelwyn area; however, their yield was far below that of the quarries at Blaenau Ffestiniog. The Welsh Highland had its administrative offices at Harbour Station on the Festiniog, but this situation changed in 1934, when, owing to pressure from shareholders, the Festiniog had to take over the Welsh Highland and operate it under a lease. The Welsh Highland, like its predecessor, had run at a loss almost from its opening in 1923 and this was a last chance to see whether anything could be done to put the books straight.

The original plan to allow Welsh Highland and Festiniog trains to run right through from Dinas to Blaenau Ffestiniog had long since gone and trains from both lines met at each side of the crossing at Porthmadog New Station. This arrangement changed yet again in 1935, when passengers had to walk through the town from Porthmadog New to the Harbour Station to catch their FR connection.

Over the years from 1923, the Colonel had experimented with internal combustion engined locomotives; however he did not find a satisfactory machine to replace the smaller 0-4-0STs used on the line, all of which were on loan from the Festiniog. The most successful locomotive was a Kerr Stuart Diesel-electric 0-6-0 which was on loan to the Company in the late 1920s; after trials the machine was sold to a sugar plantation in Mauritius, where one can still see it at work.

After two years under lease to the Festiniog

Railway it was decided to close the line, because there was no sign of financial improvement; the last passenger train ran on 26 September 1936, after which the passenger stock was stored at Dinas. The final goods train ran in May 1937 and after the departure of the last booked train, the rolling stock that remained was stored at Dinas and Beddgelert. Some stock which had been on loan had to be returned to the Festiniog. This was worked in a special train a short time after closure. Soon afterwards the crossing over the Cambrian, together with the signal cabin, was removed.

The remaining Welsh Highland rolling stock and equipment lay derelict; *Moel Tryfan* had been undergoing repair at Boston Lodge when closure took place, so the locomotive remained dismantled until cut up in 1954. Both *Russell* and the *Baldwin* were stored at Beddgelert goods shed. The Festiniog took over a number of former Welsh Highland carriages in 1936 and these vehicles are still running in a rebuilt form on the Festiniog Railway today.

The dismantling of the line took place during 1941 and early 1942, when the government requisitioned the whole undertaking for scrap metal to help the war effort. The railway was lifted in two halves, the first section from South Snowdon to Dinas, taking in the Bryngwn Branch which was completed in early 1942, and the southern portion from South Snowdon to Porthmadog New, which was completed in late 1941. In the early 1960s a Society was formed to try and re-open the line and their efforts seem to be slowly bearing fruit for they now own several locomotives and other vehicles including *Russell*, which after closure was sold to the Brymbo Steel Company and later resold to Pike Fayle & Company of Corfe Castle, Dorset. After this locomotive became redundant it was sold to the Birmingham Locomotive Club which stored it for some years at Towyn. Later the Welsh Highland Society took it over for future use on the line after restoration.

A train for Dinas runs through the Aberglaslyn pass, as a baby Austin with fabric top runs up the road from Porthmadog on the opposite side of the river. The train is made up of WHR stock and headed by an FR England 0-4-0ST. *Charles E. Lee collection*

A Dinas-bound train headed by *Russell* waits while Baldwin 590 enters Beddgelert Station with a train from Porthmadog New in the early 1930s. Already *Russell* has had its cab cut down and acquired a squat stove-pipe chimney. All these modifications were done during the abortive project to operate trains through from Dinas on the WHR to Blaenau Ffestiniog on the FR. In the picture can be seen the WHR bogie carriages in a variety of colours, for example, pink, bright yellow and green. Note also the ex-NWNGR observation car next to *Russell*. *Lens of Sutton*

Porthmadog New Station in July 1935. *Russell* simmers with a Beddgelert-bound train, while the crew passes the time in chat. Porthmadog New was a very primitive station compared with the FR's Harbour Station. New Station consisted of a collection of corrugated iron huts forming a cafe, waiting room and station office. At one time Harbour Station was closed and both FR and WHR trains used this ill-equipped place; however this changed in the early 1930s when the FR went back to operating from Harbour Station. *Real Photographs*

Baldwin 590 shunts WHR stock at Boston Lodge works in early 1936. The FR was very sophisticated in its operation compared with the WHR. Note the starting signal in background behind the Baldwin 4-6-0T. The WHR did not have signalling on the lower section relying on the staff and ticket principle and verbal instruction or handsignals throughout. However some semaphore signals were found on the former NWNGR section above Beddgelert. *Lens of Sutton*

11 THE SNAILBEACH DISTRICT RAILWAYS

The Snailbeach District Railways were promoted and built to serve the lead mines in and around the Snailbeach and Stiperstones area of Shropshire. The scheme to build the line started in 1873, when under an Act of Parliament the construction of a mineral line was authorised between Pontesbury on the GWR/LNWR joint branch to Minsterley and Snailbeach. Extensions of the line were to be authorised after the first part had been built and these included a branch from Snailbeach to Pennerley and latterly an ambitious scheme, using the 1896 Light Railways Act, to build a line to Gratten Lodge from Perkins Beach. This line would of course include a branch from Pennerley to Gravels.

The first section from Pontesbury to Snailbeach was opened to traffic in July 1877 and from the start the Company had to struggle to make ends meet. The only extensions built along the line were from the main trunk point to various lead mines, the main branch being the line from Snailbeach to Stiperstones lead mine, which was opened shortly after the main line in 1877.

One of the main promoters of the line was Sir Henry Dyke Dennis of Glyn Valley Tramway fame. Indeed, in the early days of the Snailbeach, the 0-6-0 tram locomotive *Sir Theodore* had been on loan to the line for use in construction. However, the engine kept derailing because of the difference in gauge between the

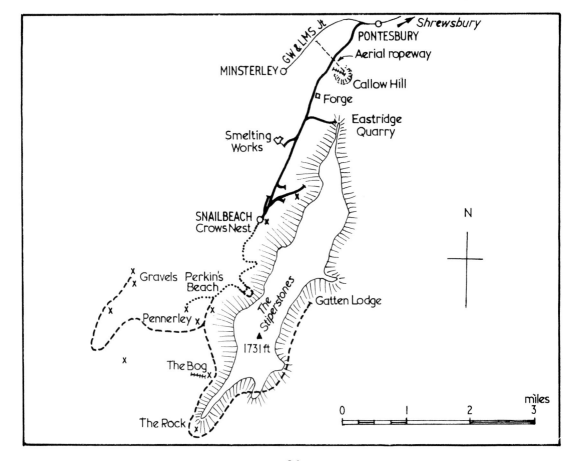

86

two lines, the GVT being 2ft 4¼in and the SDR 2ft 3¾in. Under the original management the line had three locomotives, an 0-6-0ST named *Fern Hill*, built in 1875, an 0-4-2ST named *Belmont* built by Hughes in 1873, and an 0-6-0T named *Dennis*, built by Bagnall in 1910.

The Snailbeach also had a large collection of open wagons. During the early part of the first world war the lead in the area was almost worked out but the line carried on until autumn 1915 when along with most of the mines the railway closed. The locomotives *Fernhill* and *Belmont* had been sent away to the GVT by the time of the 1915 closure, leaving only *Dennis* to work the line.

The railway was taken over by the Colonel in January 1923 and at the time of take over the whole concern was in a deplorable state. The Colonel took steps to improve matters, starting with permanent way which was relaid using heavier rail and new sleepers. He purchased 30 wagons from the War Department and three second-hand locomotives were obtained, two ex-War Department Baldwin 4-6-0Ts and the third being a *Skylark* class Kerr Stuart 0-4-2T, purchased from the Admiralty. From the reopening, the line earned much of its revenue from the quarries at Callow Hill, although there were several other sources of income.

The locomotive shed and workshop was situated at Stiperstones; here all rolling stock was repaired and overhauled.

The only original locomotive left after the Colonel's takeover was *Dennis*. He inspected this machine shortly after assuming control but he was not pleased with its condition and promptly ordered Driver Gatford, the Acting Shed Foreman, to overhaul her and get her back into traffic. However, Driver Gatford had other ideas; he hated the engine's guts and was determined not to overhaul or to operate her.

Over the next few years Gatford took *Dennis* apart very slowly. The Colonel on one occasion

even sent to Bagnalls for a copy of the drawings, which he later forwarded to Gatford in the hope that he would get weaving on the job. No such luck! Our friendly Acting Shed Foreman kept *Dennis* in bits from 1923 to 1936 when she was officially withdrawn. She was broken up slowly between 1937-1938.

The Colonel originally intended to operate passenger trains along the line, even going as far as to obtain land up to Pontesbury Station. Apart from surveying this section nothing more happened and the scheme was soon forgotten. The line bumbled along through the late 1920s and early 1930s and after the Colonel died in 1931, Austen took over the management but little changed.

The Colonel had given firm instructions that the locomotives were to be used in service for operating spells of two to three weeks only. This was good management at the time, but this order, which was adhered to long after his death, meant that all three of the operating locomotives wore out beyond repair at about the same time in 1950.

The traffic on the line ran down during the latter part of the second world war. This coupled with the fact that both the locomotives and track needed renewal made the railway uneconomic by 1946. All three locomotives were out of action with boiler defects and the Company had to use a Fordson farm tractor to tow the wagons along the line from Pontesbury to Snailbeach, the loaded vehicles being returned by gravity.

During 1947 Shropshire County Council took over the line under a lease together with the quarry at Callow Hill. The main trunk route south of Callow Hill became disused shortly after the Council take-over in 1947 and the locomotives were left to rust outside their shed at Stiperstones until the trackwork and derelict rolling stock were cleared by contractors in 1950. The northern section to Callow Hill remained in use until the autumn of 1959 when the County Council ceased to operate it. In 1961 a local scrap dealer lifted the remaining track and broke up the few remaining hopper wagons. The Tallyllyn Railway purchased some of the rail and points; however, none of the hopper wagons survived to be preserved.

Today there is still much to see of the line; narrow gauge track remains at Stiperstones near the locomotive shed, which still stands, and one can still walk the whole line from Pontesbury to Snailbeach.

Map of the Snailbeach District Railways: the solid line denotes No 1 railway actually constructed, the dotted line No 2 railway, which was not built, and the remainder the proposal under the 1896 Light Railways Act to extend from Perkins Beach to Gatten Lodge with a branch to Gravels; the crosses on the latter section represent lead mines.

Locomotives No 3 and No 2 at Stiperstones' locomotive shed in 1950 shortly after locomotive operation had ceased on the line. Both locomotives were cut up on site shortly after this photograph was taken.

Gregory Photos

SDR 0-4-2T No 2, formerly belonging to the Admiralty and sold to Colonel Stephens in 1920, is seen here at Snailbeach in 1930 on shunting duties. No 2 was a Bagnall Skylark Class 0-4-2T built to a standard design produced in the 1900s for industrial and colonial narrow gauge railways. *Real Photographs*

12 THE BURRY PORT & GWENDRAETH VALLEY RAILWAY

The Burry Port and Gwendraeth Valley Railway was opened in July 1869 from Burry Port to Pembrey embodying the earlier Kidwelly, Llanelly, and Pembrey Harbour tramroads. At first the line operated goods trains only. The original line was extended in 1891 from Burry Port to join the Llanelly & Mynydd-Mawr Railway at Sandy Gate.

The line was reconstructed as a light railway by Colonel Stephens in late 1908 and early 1909, reopening to traffic, both passenger and goods, on 2 August. It ran from Sandgate Junction on the GWR's Swansea-London main line, to Cwm Mawr, with a branch to Tycoch.

Its principal traffic was coal from the local mines, transported by rail from the pithead to Burry Port for shipment abroad. The line had originally purchased a strange collection of locomotives, which included engines built by Hughes, Fox Walker, and Robert Fairlie; after the rebuilding of the line these types were replaced by locomotives built by Peckett, Chapman & Furneaux, Avonside Engineering and Hudswell Clark, mostly side and saddle tanks, the purchase of which was authorised by the Colonel. Rolling stock consisted of former Metropolitan rigid eight-wheeler carriages plus some LSWR vehicles, and a collection of various types of goods vehicles, mostly second-hand. The stations along the line were constructed of wood, and surprisingly had running water and proper slate roofs; they also had the added luxury of gas lighting.

The Burry Port line became part of the Great Western Railway on 1 January 1923 and from the time of the grouping the Colonel had

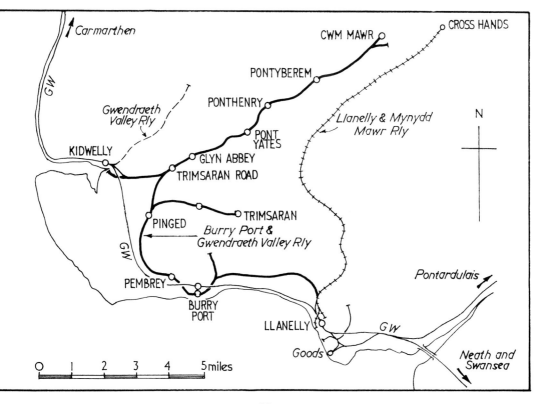

nothing further to do with the railway even though he was a member of the Board of the old company.

The Great Western later rebuilt two bogie carriages to operate the line, in addition to which the railway was the preserve of the 2021 Class 0-6-0PTs in its later years. The railway was notable for its restricted loading gauge which meant that even new bogie coaches built for the line by the GWR in 1939 had low almost flat arc roofs.

The line closed to passenger traffic on 20 September 1953. However, today a portion of the line is still open, from Llanelly, on the former GWR main line to Swansea, to Burry Port. Long may it survive to remind us of happier days.

Hudswell Clark 0-6-0T locomotive *Pioneer* at Burry Po in 1909 shortly after delivery from Leeds. The liveries the BPGV locomotives varied from locomotive t locomotive; most of the Avonside Engineering 0-6-0ST were in lined green but the Hudswell Clark locomotive were painted unlined black with burnished brass worl
LPC Ian Alla

One of the BPGV 0-6-0 saddle tanks stands at Pontyberem Station with a train of Metropolitan rigid eight-wheelers. *L&GRP*

Ponteberem and a train of ex-Metropolitan stock i 1909. The carriages consist of two Met third class rigi eight-wheelers and a Met six-wheeled carriage; at th back is a GWR four-wheeled brake van. The locomotiv depicted here is now preserved at Didcot by member of the Great Western Society who intend eventually t restore it to BPGVR livery. *LPC Ian Alla*

13 THE EDGE HILL LIGHT RAILWAY

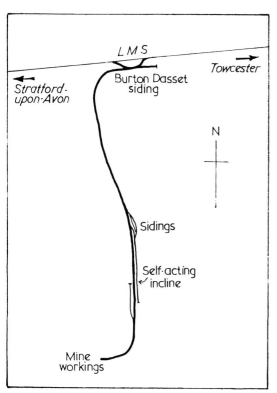

This line, built under contract by the Colonel fo a private mineral company, was promoted shortly after the first world war, in 1920, t transport minerals from the newly opened ironstone mines at Edge Hill in Oxfordshire t the sidings at Burton Dassett where the ligh railway joined the Stratford-on-Avon & Midland Junction Railway, later part of the LMS.

A strange story surrounds the line for i appears that the original plans put forward b the line's promoters were dashed when the main seams of ironstone gave out soon after the lin opened to traffic. However, the main seam o ironstone continued outside the boundaries o the mining company, but the private landowne objected to a scheme to continue mining on hi land, and so in early 1924 the workings wer closed down and the railway ceased to operate

The Edge Hill Railway was a purely minera line, and at no time were any passengers carried The rolling stock consisted of two LBSC Terrie 0-6-0Ts, one of class A1 and the other an A1X and a Manning Wardle 0-4-0 contractors' saddl tank, named *Sankey*. In addition to this th Company owned a collection of four-wheeled open wagons and two GER brake vans. Afte closure in 1925 the locomotives and rolling stock were left to rot until they were broken up along with the railway in 1947.

Abandoned stock at Edge Hill in 1945, including an ex LBSCR A1 0-6-0T, a Great Eastern Railway brake van and several four-wheeled open mineral wagons. The incline, which was rope worked, can be seen in the background. By this time the Edge Hill Railway was very desolate indeed, almost hidden from the world by weeds and dereliction.   *Lens of Sutton*

Manning Wardle 0-4-0ST *Sankey* would normally be found at the top of the incline at Edge Hill. It was stored under a road overbridge, like the other stock, which included two LBSCR 'Terriers', and a host of goods vehicles of various origins. After the line closed suddenly in the early 1920s *Sankey* was left to rot until it was cut up in 1946 with the rest of the rolling stock.

L&GRP

Edge Hill 0-6-0T No 1, formerly LBSCR No 73 *Deptford*. Although this engine, seen here in 1930s, had been out of use for some years it was not scrapped until 1946.

L&GRP

14 THE NORTH DEVON & CORNWALL JUNCTION RAILWAY

The North Devon & Cornwall Junction Railway was the last standard gauge line to be constructed by the Colonel. The railway ran from Torrington, on the Southern's branch to Bude, to Halwill Junction on the Southern's branch to Wadebridge. The railway was constructed by an independent company in much the same way as the Sheppey Light Railway. This scheme was put into effect partly to relieve unemployment in the West Country in the early 1920s.

It was opened to traffic on 27 July 1925 and from the opening the Southern Railway operated the line on behalf of the Company.

However the line was never owned by the Southern Railway, and did not become part of the Southern system proper until after nationalisation in 1948, when it was taken into the Southern Region. In 1963 all Southern Region lines west of Salisbury were handed over to the Western Region which closed it on 1 March 1965 to passenger traffic, but the line is still open to Meeth for china clay traffic.

The North Devon & Cornwall line incorporated part of the 3ft gauge Torrington & Marland Mineral Tramway. The station buildings along the line were very similar to those on the K&ESR, and were constructed of corrugated iron and wood, although some were built of local stone. Motive power was in the form of rebuilt E1R 0-6-2Ts which had been specially reconstructed by R. E. L. Maunsell at Eastleigh for operating in the West of England and O2 0-4-4Ts working rail motor sets. Later this changed to LMR type Ivatt 2-6-2Ts and corridor stock.

The line served the farming community of the north western part of Devon and Cornwall and, like most rural lines of its type, it was a victim of the Beeching Plan in the early 1960s.

Top:
A Torrington & Marland Mineral Railway train crosses a timber trestle near Marland in 1912. This 3ft gauge line was built in 1880 to connect various quarries with the jetty at Torrington; the locomotive is an 0-6-0ST and the train consists of empty four-wheeled short-wheelbase open wagons. The tramway was later converted to standard gauge by Colonel Stephens in 1923.
Author's collection

Right:
A Class E1R 0-6-2T and an ex LSWR push-pull coach cross a viaduct near Torrington in 1935. The photograph shows the construction of the brick and steel girder bridge. *LCGB Ken Nunn collection*

15 THE PLYMOUTH, DEVONPORT & SOUTH WESTERN JUNCTION RAILWAY

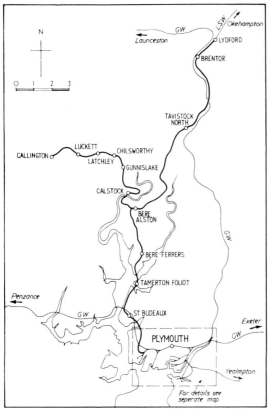

The Plymouth, Devonport & South Western Junction Railway, Callington section, was opened to traffic on 2 March 1908. The line, which had been promoted privately by an independent company outside the LSWR, ran from Bere Alston to Callington. However, the Company was on very good terms with the Board of the LSWR from the opening and trains had running rights between Bere Alston and Plymouth.

The section of line from the northern end of Calstock Viaduct to Gunnislake was built on the alignment of the former East Cornwall Mineral Railway, formerly a 3ft 6in gauge mineral tramway, opened in 1872 and which at one time served the local tin mines in the area. The East Cornwall line was taken over in 1894. During the time of the PD&SWJR's construction most of the mineral line was abandoned. The PD&SWJR served the tin mining and quarrying industries of the Tamar Valley, most of the traffic from which was channelled through Calstock where a wagon lift was built on to the

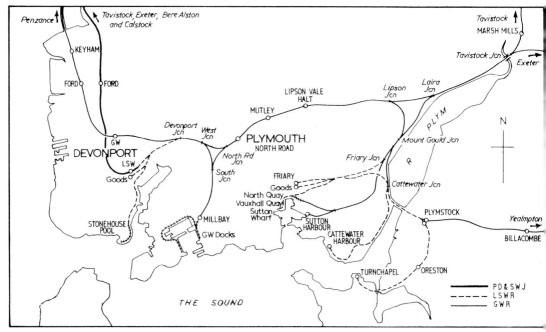

viaduct to serve the wharves from the main line.

According to Colonel Stephens, Calstock Viaduct over the Tamar was as deep in its foundations as it was in its height. He served the Company as engineer of works during construction of the line, and after the line's opening in 1908, he became the Company's resident manager. One of the stipulations of the Colonel's contract stated that in order to hold down the position he should be on hand for three days of the week to supervise the line's operation. As he was hardly ever on hand to do his job, the Board asked him to resign only a year after the line had opened.

The line became a part of the LSWR in early 1922, and was grouped into the Southern a year later. Things did not change much during Southern days, but a number of changes took place after nationalisation in 1948, when permanent way and signalling were renewed; in 1958 the line became part of the Western Region. Part of the line, from Gunnislake to Callington, was closed on 5 November 1966, leaving the section from Bere Alston to Gunnislake still open to passenger traffic, and indeed today providing the only passenger service on the former LSWR route out of Plymouth.

The railway had a handsome stud of three Hawthorn Leslie tank locomotives, of which two were 0-6-2Ts of a design not unlike K&ESR No 4 *Hecate*, in their body outline. The third machine was an 0-6-0T, again not unlike a K&ESR 2-4-0 in its outline. All three were named, the 0-6-2Ts being *Earl of Mount Edgcumbe* and *Earl St Leven*, the 0-6-0T receiving the name *A. S. Harris*.

The Company owned a fourth locomotive in the early days of the line, a former East Cornwall Mineral Railway 0-4-0ST converted from 3ft 6in gauge to standard gauge. This machine was used to shunt the yard at Callington but was later sold to Colonel Stephens for use on the Selsey Tramway along with the two former LSWR royal saloons, one of which went to the K&ESR and the other to the Shropshire & Montgomeryshire line.

The passenger rolling stock consisted of a set of eight North London Railway four-wheeled vehicles, which were replaced after a number of years with LSWR vehicles. A six-wheeled goods brake van was unusual for it incorporated a passenger compartment for quarry workers.

After the Southern takeover in 1923, the four-wheelers were replaced with LSWR gate push-pull trailers. The 0-6-0T *A. S. Harris* went far from home, among other places to Clapham Junction and Ashford. It was replaced by an O2

Earl St Leven at the head of a train of ex-LSWR four-wheeled coaches at Callington in 1911; in the background is the train shed. At this time a local train service was run between Callington and Calstock, in addition to trains for Bere Alston and Plymouth.
Lens of Sutton

0-4-4T on passenger trains. The 0-6-2Ts however remained in the district until the mid-1950s when they went to Eastleigh Works for scrapping, being replaced by Ivatt 2-6-2Ts of LMS design.

The station buildings along the line were very similar to Tenterden Town Station in design, except that in some cases the buildings were on island platforms with awnings at each side. At Callington there was a train shed which covered most of the platform.

The erstwhile PD&SWJR is now the furthest west that can be reached on the former Southern system. One of the main reasons for the retention of the last portion of the line is that the railway provides a lifeline across the River Tamar since there are no direct main roads between Gunnislake, Calstock and Plymouth. For the moment therefore the line continues to operate as a basic railway, in almost modern Stephens form.

Plymouth, Devonport & South Western Junction Railway locomotives at Callington shed in 1909, showing *Earl of Mount Edgcumbe*. At the head of two open wagons behind, *Earl St Leven* can be seen in the engine shed. The locomotives were painted blue at this time, but later the livery changed to a style similar to that used on the LSWR. *LPC Ian Allan*

Calstock viaduct shortly after the opening of the line in 1908 showing the wagon lift on the far left, which served an industrial complex on the west bank of the Tamar. *W. H. Austen collection TRC*

Bottom right:
A general view of Gunnislake Station in Southern Railway days showing the island platform and goods yard. Today with the bare minimum of facilities it is the terminus of a service from Plymouth and is the only one of the former Colonel Stephens' lines which came into the BR network to retain a passenger service. *L&GRP*

16 THE SHEPPEY LIGHT RAILWAY

Eastchurch Station in 1950, showing the building and track layout. The building is a typical example of a Colonel Stephens' corrugated iron structure, with its extended awning and supports using v-shaped joints at the top. Note the gas lamps on the station platform and the concrete platform facing. *Lens of Sutton*

The Sheppey Light Railway was constructed by the Colonel on behalf of an independent company. The line was opened to traffic on 1 August 1901, and ran from Queenborough on the SE&CR's Sheerness-Port Victoria branch to Leysdown on the east coast of the Island.

From the opening, the line was operated by the South Eastern & Chatham on the Company's behalf. Motive power was normally provided in the form of a Kitson rail motor, or for goods traffic an ex-LBSCR A1 0-6-0T purchased secondhand by the SE&CR for working the line. In the years after the SE&CR assumed control on 31 October 1905 the line was operated using class P 0-6-0T and R1 0-4-4Ts, coupled to auto trailers or converted former railmotor carriages articulated in pairs.

The station buildings along the line were very much like buildings on the Colonel's other railways and were constructed of corrugated iron with wood framing. The line made very little money for the original company, and still less for the SE&CR. Even though the railway was a white elephant the Southern continued to run the line through its time and it was not finally closed until 3 December 1950, only three years after nationalisation.

SECR railcar No 1, shortly after being outshopped in 1901 and used from the early days of the line. These rail motors were withdrawn just before the first world war, the carriage portions being converted for normal locomotive working as push-pull sets, some articulated in pairs.   *BR*

17   THE PADDOCKWOOD & HAWKHURST RAILWAY

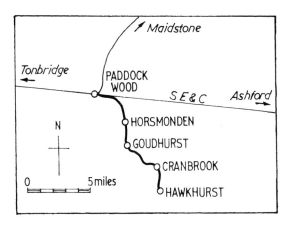

The Paddockwood & Hawkhurst Railway was the Colonel's first project at the early age of 22. The line was originally intended as a branch to connect Paddockwood to Rye, for which plans were made in 1845; however, nothing came of this first scheme, and other projects of a similar nature were put forward in the following years until 1864 when the South Eastern Railway, concerned over its position in the area, supported local promoters to project a line from Paddockwood to Cranbrook. At this time also a

separate company was formed to build a line from Cranbrook to Tenterden.

Work started on the line's construction in 1879 but soon stopped for financial reasons. After a short period the South Eastern Railway assumed control of the company but little happened until work started in earnest in 1891 with Stephens in charge of every aspect of construction. On 1 October 1892, the line was opened as far as Hope Mill, later renamed Goudhurst. This was followed a year later on 4 September by the continuation to Hawkhurst.

The railway was projected as a private local company which handed over the line to the South Eastern Railway on completion of the works. The main traffic was fruit and hops, which were transported to London from most stations. Most stations were some distance from the villages they served which did not help the line as far as passenger traffic was concerned. The route was difficult in some respects; the gradients were steep between Goudhurst and Cranbrook, the steepest being 1 in 60, and the line boasted a short tunnel near Cranbrook. The branch had a very uneventful life but had quite a variety of motive power during its time. In South

Eastern days Cudworth 2-4-0s and other small types were used; in Southern days a number of SECR and LBSCR locomotives were seen on the branch, among them Chatham R1 0-4-4Ts, SEC H Class 0-4-4Ts, C Class 0-6-0s, Brighton E1 0-6-0Ts and E4 0-6-2Ts. Even Brighton C2X 0-6-0s were tried for a short time, and surprisingly, larger classes of 4-4-0 tender locomotives were used as well, mostly on weekend excursion traffic.

The station buildings were quite interesting for they varied tremendously. Goudhurst was a substantial brick building, while Horsmonden and Hawkhurst stations were typical Colonel Stephens' corrugated-iron buildings. Cranbrook was a brick and timber structure of a plainer pattern when compared with Goudhurst. The line never really made a profit and it was not surprising that towards the later 1950s, British Railways took the first steps towards closure.

Branch train formations had remained much the same since early Southern days, with 0-4-4Ts working push-pull sets, and the occasional school specials using main line corridor stock, and the hop pickers' trains.

A Class C 0-6-0 works a pick-up freight near Cranbrook in early June 1961. The Hawkhurst branch handled a large proportion of the local fruit and hop traffic until closure in June 1961. Other classes used on the line at this time varied from H Class 0-4-4Ts to L1 4-4-0 tender locomotives. *D. Cobbe collection*

The line's final closure came on 6 June 1961, the same day as the neighbouring Kent & East Sussex branch. The last train was an enthusiasts' special, organised by the LCGB. However it was a number of years before contractors lifted the track and demolished the works. Today little is left to provide reminders of the branch, for most of the station buildings have gone and little remains of the course of the line.

Hawkhurst Station in 1956 showing the corrugated iron station building typical of Stephens' designs with the wooden supports under the awning. The gas lamps are quite ornate with their twirly main castings and the station name in the glass above the lantern. Note the tight run-round loop which could accommodate an L1 4-4-0; the carriages in the bay are former LSWR corridor vehicles some of which were originally used for emigrant traffic. Later they were converted for local push-pull workings by the Southern Railway.
Lens of Sutton

18 THE PETROL RAILBUSES

The Wolseley Sidley being unloaded at Chichester on the Selsey Tramway about 1920. The car ran on this line coupled to a rail lorry. Later, after being involved in an accident, it was laid aside and then sent to Kinnerley on the S&M where its body was used to refurbish the trailer for *Gazelle*.   *E. C. Griffith*

The Wolseley Sidley chassis before the fitting of the railcar body at Rolvenden about 1919. Later a body was built by Drake & Fletcher of Maidstone. At this time the vehicle was used as a goods tractor.

F. H. Smith collection

Railbus luggage trolley at Rolvenden in 1947, used at this time for ballasting track by PW staff.

J. Norris collection

The K&ESR Shefflex set at Headcorn in 1934. It had been delivered in 1930 and was used extensively over the line until 1938 when it was withdrawn and sold in 1941.
H. C. Casserley

...-works at Chichester on the Selsey tramway in 1923, ... Ford two-car set and luggage trolley. This set worked ... the line until the end of services in 1935. Later a ...hefflex two-car set was also purchased to supplement ...rvice on the line. Note the chilled cast wheels with ...aped spokes.
W. H. Austen TRC

...he S&M three-car set of 1923 here seen in ex-works ...ondition. Contrary to popular belief the chassis of this ...t was not built by Fords, but a subsidiary American ...mpany under contract from Ford during the first ...orld war. The set ran as a three-car unit for a time in ...e early 1920s after which it became a two-car set until ...33 when the line closed to passenger traffic. It was ...oken up in late 1935 at Kinnerley.
W. H. Austen TRC

Above:
PD&SWJR 0-6-2T *Earl of Mount Edgcumbe* at Callington in 1908. Unlike the other Hawthorn tanks so far described this engine and its sister were fitted with Belpaire fireboxes. Both PD&SWJR 0-6-2Ts survived well into BR days and latterly in the late 1950s operated at Eastleigh works on shunting duties.

W. H. Austen collection

Bottom right:
S&M 0-6-2T at Kinnerley in 1912, one of two 0-6-2Ts purchased by the Colonel for the S&M. Later, just before the outbreak of the first world war both 0-6-2Ts were sold to the Woolmer Instructional Military Railway, later the Longmoor Military Railway.

LPC Ian Allan

Below:
PD&SWJR 0-6-0T *A. S. Harris*, here seen at Nine Elms in 1934. This engine was purchased to operate the passenger service on the PD&SWJR. However, after the Southern takeover in 1923 the locomotive soon moved to the London area where it worked as a shed and carriage pilot. *H. C. Casserley*

Top right:
Rother Valley Railway 2-4-0T No 2 *Northiam* of 1899 a Rolvenden Shed in 1906, showing the locomotive with its original chimney before the stovepipe was fitted Later, sister locomotive No 1 *Tenterden* was rebuilt with 4ft 1in driving wheels, purchased, it is believed, from the SE&CR. Both engines operated until the late 1930 when they were withdrawn and later sold for scrap, No 2 meanwhile, as mentioned earlier, having been in the Will Hay film, *Oh, Mr Porter*. *W. H. Austen collectio*

19 THE COLONEL'S HAWTHORNS

Right:
K&ESR 0-8-0T No 4 *Hecate*, built in 1904 for use or through trains over the main line between Headcorn and Tonbridge. This service never materialised, and as far as can be ascertained *Hecate* was used only once a year, during Biddenden fair week, to move the large amount of cattle traffic. In 1932 the KESR arranged an exchange with the Southern Railway for LSWR 0-6-0ST No 335 and two spare boilers. In Southern and early BR days *Hecate* worked from Nine Elms on carriage shunting duties at Clapham Junction until it was scrapped in 1950. *W. H. Austen collection*

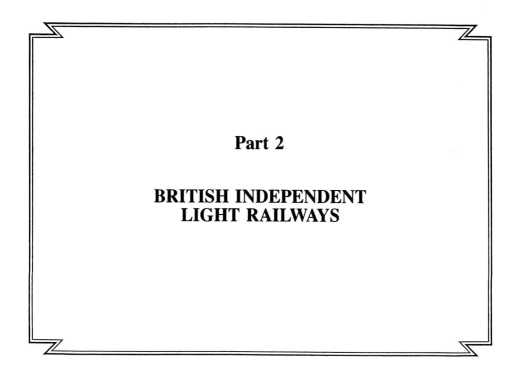

Part 2

BRITISH INDEPENDENT
LIGHT RAILWAYS

Edwin Lambert '79

The Railways of Arcadia

Through the leafy avenues of trees that flank the Onney Valley there once ran a railway, its tracks of tarnished orange-red steel, like thin strips, penetrating the grass-choked ballast bed. The sun, piercing the few gaps in the green ceiling above, beat down in a blaze of afternoon heat. Across the river, towards Craven Arms, a sound could just be discerned, and, presently, in the distance, there was a wisp of white vapour above the trees. Over the River Onney, its waters clear and almost transparent, the sound of a steam locomotive could be heard as a train made its way up the winding valley to Lydham Heath, under the trees and past the hedgerows dividing the fields on each side. Then it could be seen. The sun glistened on her polished brass and burnished copper cap; *Carlisle* was her name, proud and defiant, ancient but very beautiful.

She plodded her way through the undergrowth with elegance and grace, hauling a string of old and battered four-wheel coaches behind her. Away now towards her destination, late as usual, but possessing a human warmth that will always be a part of these rolling hills of Shropshire. The scene was timeless, without a tomorrow, where yesterday was everything, seemingly for ever.

A long time ago, long before preservation societies were thought of, the light railways of Britain provided the adventure for those in search of romance. Across Britain light railways could be found from Lee-on-the-Solent to North Sunderland, and from Mid Suffolk to Liskeard. They had a wonderful character, enhanced by their idyllic charm. On these lines one could find a wonderful mixture of locomotives and rolling stock. Indeed it was not unknown for a train of ancient decrepit four- and six-wheelers to be hauled by a large modern 2-6-0 or heavy 0-6-2T.

Left: One of the railways of Arcadia, the Bishops Castle Railway. A mixed train headed by *Carlisle*, built by Kitson & Co of Leeds in 1868, portrayed here around 1900. (*Edwin Lambert*)

Carriages came in all shapes and sizes, mostly second or even third hand. Few companies had new or original carriage stock after the first decade of existence. Some lines had rather square very ancient four-wheel stock, not far removed from the stage coach era, while others had elegant bogie vehicles. Wagons, too, came in a strange mixture, not only opens and vans of former main line origin, but also a large assortment of odds and ends which consisted of permanent way vehicles and non-passenger carriage stock.

Whatever the fascination of the rolling stock, it was the railways themselves and their staff that held most interest. The staff were mainly local rural folk recruited from farming communities, underpaid, often overworked, but usually a contented bunch. On lines like the Bishops Castle the management was always frightened of ridicule; how short sighted they were, for they could not see that the interest generated by individuals was largely due to a genuine affection for the line and, not as it thought, a back-handed dig at the system.

For those who loved the odd and the Bohemian, there were many lines to choose. The Spurn Head had platelayers' trolleys propelled by sails; the Bishops Castle, had its unseasoned tree trunk sleepers that took sprout, complete with roots, and turned into new trees, while on the Wantage Tramway, there was the ancient England 0-4-0T *Jane*, which escaped the scrap merchant's torch on many occasions and happily today, more than 100 years old, is at Didcot GWS Depot restored to working order.

The history of the railway network which, until the early 1960s, ran to most parts of the British Isles, connecting its main centres with ports and key locations of industry, stems from the 1830s to the 1850s, for it was at that time in industrial history that our railway network began the development to its peak of importance.

By the 1870s and mid-1880s more obscure locations were being reached by branch lines, mostly promoted either directly by main line railways or small independent companies formed to build a local line, after which the branch would be contracted out and worked by a main line company on the local concern's behalf.

It was not until the Light Railways Act of 1896 that small local companies, owned and operated by local people, became more of a reality, though some lines were built as light railways under earlier Acts. This was due partly to an official relaxation by the Board of Trade of stringent rules and regulations for railway promotion, construction, and operation, and the setting up of the Light Railway Commission to look into light railway projects in general; the commissioners went up and down the country evaluating light railway proposals on the strength of which Light Railway Orders were refused or granted. This body ceased to exist in the post first world war period, its powers then being vested in the Board of Trade.

We have already dealt with one group of lines promoted in this period around the turn of the century in a previous volume (*The Colonel Stephens Railways*, David & Charles 1978). This present book looks at other standard gauge independent light railways promoted and built by small companies, with local finance, and whose main aim in life was to serve a given local community or industry.

In the main these light railways were promoted in the late 1890s or early 1900s, using both local and borrowed capital from various financial institutions. Few ever made any profit for the shareholders or companies concerned. Most were bankrupt by the late 1920s or early 1930s and in the hands of an official receiver. Local businessmen and others who, full of hope, put money into these risky projects, soon found that they were throwing good money after bad, and as the years went by saw their share values get lower and lower. In some cases the shareholders managed either to persuade a main line company to purchase or group the unremunerative line into its concern, while others managed to hire motive power and stock from those same main line companies. Less fortunate companies bumbled on from one year to the next and from one crisis to the next, until finally the whole concern died a natural death.

Today, there is little left to show what the independent light railways looked like. One of the few lines still partly in use, but in totally different fashion from its promoters' intentions, is the Corringham Light Railway, which today carries block oil trains at Thames Haven. Another is the Derwent Valley Light Railway at York which survives under the control of the original company. Today it is a freight only line, an attempt to run tourist steam passenger trains in the late 1970s having proved unsuccessful. The only line today still with a passenger service is the Liskeard & Looe, now a BR 'basic railway' branch which might even assume a greater importance if park-and-ride schemes are evolved at Liskeard to cope with Looe holiday traffic.

The British independent light railway was in itself the epitomy of British eccentricity. It was a mixture of dedicated management and staff who, through thick and thin, against all realistic odds, tried to provide remote rural districts with a good basic service, and well meaning individuals who did what they earnestly thought was right. Equally, though, it was a mixture of beauty, rustic rural charm, and awesome wonder.

20 LISKEARD, CARADON & LOOE RAILWAY

The Liskeard & Looe line had its origins in the Liskeard & Looe Union Canal opened in the late 1820s from Moorswater to Looe Harbour. Later the rail link to Caradon mines, to the north of Liskeard, was built by the Liskeard & Caradon Railway and opened in 1844. At first it was worked by horses and served the tin and copper mines around Caradon Mill with a number of feeder branch lines. The railway and canal companies were separate undertakings but inevitably their operations were closely interwoven. The LCR undertook further extensions in 1840s from Caradon to Cheesewring granite quarry, to Gonamena, and in 1861 to Tokenbury. In 1860 the company purchased the already established Kilmar horse tramway. By now there was 12 miles of horse tramway and $6\frac{3}{4}$

miles of canal, but the canal company decided to build a rail connection between Moorswater and Looe Harbour, opened in December 1860 for mineral traffic thus avoiding the need to trans-ship good at Moorswater from rail to canal. The canal and new railway ran side by side from Moorswater for most of the way to Looe. The two companies also formed a joint working committee to concentrate operation in a single management. At first the new railway to Looe was worked as a horse tramway but was converted to locomotive operation in 1862, only two years after construction. The locomotive shed and workshops were at Moorswater, in a long stone shed. Moorswater, it should be noted, was situated right down in the valley of the East Looe river, about $\frac{1}{2}$ mile from Liskeard set high above on the hillside

L&LR 0-6-OST *Cheesewring* shunts open wagons at Moorswater under the GWR viaduct about 1901. At this point wagons of quarried stone and tin ore were shunted onto the loop opened in 1901 to be transferred to the Great Western at Liskeard. (*Ken Nunn courtesy LCGB*)

to the east. This geographical relationship affected the later history of the line when connections with the outside world were planned.

To work the lines, the railway purchased over a period of seven years three 0-6-0STs named *Caradon, Cheesewring* and *Kilmar* from Gilkes Wilson and their successors Hopkins Gilkes. The Liskeard & Caradon which had taken a lease of the Looe section started to run passenger trains between Moorswater and Looe in 1879 with operation under light railway requirements of the 1868 Regulation of Railways Act.

By the turn of the century the Liskeard & Looe Railway, as it was now known, was feeling its isolation for there had been nothing but financial problems. Plans were evolved to build an extension from Moorswater up to Liskeard Great Western station high up nearer the town. Several schemes were devised, including a possible rack railway, but the one actually built left the Looe line, facing from Caradon, near Moorswater to climb steeply out of the valley, under Liskeard GW viaduct and then with a horseshoe turn to reach the GWR station from the north east. The extension was opened in May 1901 and really turned the line into a branch off the main line.

The finances were still not good and in 1909 the Looe and Caradon lines were taken over by the GWR. The Caradon line closed in 1917 as the mines ceased production but the Looe line continued, though trains to and from Liskeard had to reverse at Moorswater.

In 1907 the L&LR had purchased a very attractive 2-4-0T, a Barclay product named *Lady Margaret*, later numbered 1308 by the GWR. After re-boilering this locomotive travelled far away to the Cambrian section of the GWR after 1923. Two of the three Gilkes 0-6-0STs were inherited by the GWR. *Cheesewring* became 1311 and *Kilmar* 1312 which lasted until the first world war years. Another engine 0-6-0ST *Looe* delivered in 1901 ended its days in the London Docks. *Looe* was not successful and was replaced in 1902 by GW 4-4-0ST No 13 which was hired until the GWR takeover, and remained for 20 years.

At the turn of the century the railway had a rake of antique four-wheel coaches from the early days of the passenger service. By 1907 however, the line had a number of ex-Mersey Railway long wheelbase four-wheelers comprising thirds, brake thirds and composites. There were also some end balcony bogie saloon coaches originally bought new from Hurst Nelson in 1901 but sold in 1904

although they remained on the line for two more years, when two of the three were badly damaged in a collision with a runaway train.

Station buildings were provided at Coombe, St Keyne, Causeland, Sandplace and Looe, the buildings being of wood and stone construction. Until the GWR takeover in 1909, the company had little or no signalling. However, the GWR installed signals of its standard types along the line.

The goods rolling stock consisted of a large number of short wheelbase four-wheel open wagons. The company also had a four-wheel brake van No 1 and low sided wagons.

After 1923 the GWR operated class 45XX 2-6-2Ts and Dean 0-6-0STs of the 1854 class. Since the 1960s the line has been worked by diesel multiple-units based at Plymouth. Although the Looe branch has been threatened with closure on several occasions it has not actually happened and there is even talk of boosting rail services to Looe by a park-and-ride scheme from Liskeard to try and reduce car traffic at Looe in the summer holiday period.

Top: After the GWR take over in 1909 0-6-0ST *Kilmar* shunts wagons at Moorswater yard to form a mixed train for Liskeard exchange sidings. (*Rev E. R. Boston collection*)

Centre: 0-6-0ST *Caradon* at Looe in 1900. The locomotives built for this line were constructed by Hopkins & Gilks which also produced some of the parts of the Tay Bridge which collapsed in 1879. Note the attractive heavy black and orange lining, also the ornate chimney with its copper cap. The firebox from this locomotive still exists at Didcot Railway Centre, in the museum collection (*Lens of Sutton*)

Right: In 1907 the Company ordered a new locomotive from Barclays. This little 2-4-0T named *Lady Margaret* was used on passenger trains until about 1910 when it went to Swindon for rebuilding with a Dean type boiler and other GWR fittings. It ran for a few more years on the Looe branch before going north to Oswestry on the former Cambrian where it worked the Tanat Valley Light Railway with two older ex-Cambrian Sharp Stewart 2-4-0T. It finally cut up in 1947. (*Lens of Sutton*)

21 BIDEFORD, WESTWARD HO & APPLEDORE

The Bideford, Westward Ho & Appledore was perhaps one of the most unusual of the British light railways. It was a street tramway operated by steam traction, but unlike most of the lines so far described it was isolated from its nearest neighbour, the LSWR line from Barnstaple to Torrington. Even though it was a standard gauge railway, its stock had centre couplers like a narrow gauge line.

Opened in May 1901 the railway ran from Bideford Quay to Appledore via Westward Ho, a distance of some seven miles. The company was owned by the British Electric Traction Group, and for this reason alone it was quite unusual that such a line opened at such a late date with steam traction.

The tramway had a fleet of three identical Hunslet 2-4-2Ts, named *Granville*, *Torridge* and *Kingsley*, although it is hard to find any trace of these names on any photographs of the locomotives. It also had six bogie balcony-end saloons which ran in pairs in summer and as single

cars at other less busy times. In addition the tramway had some goods vehicles which included open wagons and a brake van. The line had no stations as such for it picked up passengers at roadside stops, although shelters were provided at some locations. It also made little or no money, and BET was not amused by it. After 1914 BET had a good excuse to rid itself of this white elephant of a system, and the last train ran on 23 March 1917. Shortly after, all three locomotives were sold to the Ministry of Munitions for further use, although they did not go far, for Nos 1 and 3, after conversion to conventional buffers and couplings, were used as shunting locomotives at Pembrey Ordnance Depot and No 2 was used for similar work at Avonmouth Ordnance Depot.

In December 1918 No 3 was sold to the South Met Gas Co. The permanent way and the rest of the rolling stock was sold for scrap in early 1918 and was removed by the beginning of 1919. Today, little remains of the line and the tramway has joined the ranks of Britain's lost railways.

Top: A BWHA train stands waiting to leave Bideford Promenade for Appledore in 1909. (*Lens of Sutton*)

Centre: No 2 heads out of Bideford, past the Monument and through the main street in Autumn of 1911. In summer, trains consisted of two bogie saloons; in winter, only one was used on each train.

Below: A 2-4-2 tram tank heads out towards Westward Ho, through the countryside between the fields and behind the hedgerows in 1910. (*Photomatic*)

Bottom Right: Arrival at Bideford Quay in 1901 showing clearly a bogie carriage with its full lettering and coat of arms. (*Lens of Sutton*)

22 WEST SOMERSET MINERAL RAILWAY

The WSMR was built primarily as a mineral line carrying iron ore for the Ebbw Vale Steel Company and served the Brendon Hill iron mine. At the site of the mine the company built a $\frac{3}{4}$ mile double track 1 in 4 cable incline from the mine to the railway. It was opened in September 1859, and ran from Gupworthy to Watchet Harbour, 12 miles distant.

A passenger service operated on the 'main' line, using a collection of four-wheeled stock bought new at the opening. Stations were built of local stone, with stone platforms, timber awnings and slate roofs. The line was fully signalled using disc-and-crossbar signals.

The Ebbw Vale Steel Co supplied two long-boiler Sharp Stewart 0-6-0s and two Sharp Stewart outside framed 0-6-0STs. Later the Ebbw Vale Co sold both the 0-6-0STs and one of the long boiler 0-6-0s. All four were named, *Rowcliffe*, *Pontypool*, *Brendon* and *Atlas*. In addition the WSMR owned two Nelson-built 0-4-0 box tanks, which worked on the top of the incline at the mine workings.

The original owners decided in 1898 to close the mine and railway but after closure a syndicate was formed to purchase and run the concern, and for a short time from 1907 operated it with an ex-Metropolitan 4-4-0T and some contractors wagons. The new owners went bankrupt within a year or two but the line was used for one more event when the Angus Co of New Zealand used a section near Watchet for signal experiments in 1909, after which the track was lifted during the first world war.

Top left: The Mineral Syndicate's ex-Metropolitan 4-4-0T No 37 posed for an official photograph at Roadwater in July 1907. (*L&GRP courtesy David & Charles*)

Above: The incline at Brendon which led up to the mine, after abandonment, about 1900. (*Ken Nunn courtesy LCGB*)

Bottom left: Later the same day at the foot of the Brendon incline decked in flags and banners. (*L&GRP courtesy David & Charles*)

Below: Roadwater station, about 1912, after the A. R. Angus Co had used the site for brake experiments a ramp for which can be seen between the rails. (*Ken Nunn courtesy LCGB*)

23   LEE-ON-THE-SOLENT LIGHT RAILWAY

One of the most obscure light railways of all time is the best way to describe the Lee-on-the-Solent line. Opened in May 1894 from Fort Brockhurst on the Fareham–Gosport branch to Lee-on-the-Solent, a distance of three miles, its permanent way was very light, being laid in 40 lb flat-bottom rail spiked to wooden sleepers. Stations along the line were very crude wooden halts with sleeper-built platforms.

The company owned no locomotives or stock of its own, having to hire them from the LSWR which loaned two former contractors tank engines to work the line, one an England-built 2-4-0T named *Scott*, the other an 0-6-0ST named *Lady Portsmouth* built by Manning Wardle. Both handled the service until the first world war, when the LSWR then loaned an ex-LBSCR A1 class 0-6-0T which had been used previously on the Lyme Regis

branch. Carriage stock came in the form of LSWR four- and six-wheel coaches and a full brake van. All the goods stock came from outside main line companies, temporarily borrowed while in transit.

The old company ceased to exist as an independent entity in 1923, when it became part of the Southern Railway. It did not have a long future, though, for in 1932 the line closed to passengers. By this time the SR was using ex-SECR P class 0-6-0Ts and ex-LBSCR D1 0-4-2Ts on the trains with ex-LSWR motor trailers for passenger services.

In 1934 the line closed altogether and the track was lifted during the following year. Today little remains of the former railway and it is hard to find remains. However the station at Lee-on-the-Solent is still intact and used partly as a shop and also forms part of the bus station.

24   LAMBOURN VALLEY RAILWAY

The Lambourn Valley had a very short independent history. It opened as a light railway in 1901 between Newbury and Lambourn, and served the local agricultural community and the horse racing fraternity at Lambourn.

Originally the company had a fleet of teak painted balcony end four-wheel coaches and three 0-6-0Ts, two built by Chapman Fulgurex and a third by Hunslet of Leeds. All three were painted royal blue and were named *Aelfred*, *Eahlswith* and *Eadweade*, after personalities in the Alfred legends, painted in the old English style of lettering. They were taken over by the GWR becoming Nos 820, 821 and 819. The new owners used steam railmotors and, later, auto trains on the line. The branch survived grouping, and nationalisation, but lost its passenger service in January 1960, and was closed to freight in June 1973.

The original buildings were of timber and brick but later, after the GWR took over, some standard GWR type buildings appeared. Most of the original buildings had gone by the late 1920s. In the early days half tree trunk sleepers and flat bottom rail were used.

At first the company hired a tank locomotive No 1384, a 2-4-0T, from the GWR before its own locomotives arrived. No 1384 later went to the Weston, Clevedon & Portishead Railway where it became No 4, until it was cut up in 1940. In 1904 the LVR company sold its line to the Great Western, which was very quick to change things to GWR standards.

In its last years a service was worked for the American Air Force base at Welford Park. A few relics of the line are preserved at Didcot railway centre, including the original ticket office from Welford Park Station.

Above: The Lee-on-the-Solent Light Railway. A Stroudley Class E 0-6-0T of the LBSCR is pictured with a train at Lee-on-the-Solent in 1928. (*Edwin Lambert*)

Right: Former Lambourn Valley Hunslet-built 0-6-0T *Eadweade* after sale to the Cambrian in 1910, at Oswestry works yard. By this time it bore GWR lettering and a Cambrian number, 24. It became GWR property in 1923 again. Both its companion LVR engines were sold for use in industry. (*LPC courtesy Ian Allan*)

Below: Lambourn Valley 0-6-0T *Eahlswith*, rolls past the round frame at Newbury in 1901. LVR locomotives were painted an attractive shade of dark blue, and stock was equally attractive in natural wood. The original stock did not last long after the GWR takeover in 1904. The locomotives went to the Cambrian Railways and the stock to the Selsey Tramway. (*LPC courtesy Ian Allan*)

25 WANTAGE TRAMWAY

The Wantage Tramway was one of Britain's most famous light railways, for it typified the roadside rural tramway concept used extensively in Ireland and in Europe but not often in Britain. Using a route from Wantage Road station on the GWR's London and Bristol main line it ran for 2¾ miles to Wantage town and was of standard gauge. It served the local community with a tram service to the main line station, and also served a dairy and other minor local industries and agriculture in the district.

The company was incorporated in 1874 and the line opened in October 1875 as the first steam tramway in the country. It had a variety of interesting vehicles, ranging from a Merryweather steam tram, built in 1872, and a Falcon 0-4-0 tram locomotive of 1876, to a more conventional 0-4-0ST, built by Manning Wardle in 1888, and most famous of all, No 5 0-4-0WT *Jane*, built in 1857 by George England & Co.

Apart from No 5 the treasure of the line was No 6, an 0-4-0 tram locomotive built by Matthews, the only one of its type built by this firm. For passenger accommodation the line used a number of ex-Reading horse trams, adapted for locomotive use, and a bogie tram.

There were no stations as passengers were picked up on route. The workshops were at Wantage, in a collection of wooden buildings, but heavy repairs had to be carried out at Swindon GWR works. For much of its life the company found it hard to make ends meet, but especially after the first world war, with the advent of the motor bus.

In August 1925 the company withdrew passenger services but freight services continued and complete closure did not come until the end of 1945. During the second world war the American army unwittingly damaged the track by parking heavy army vehicles on the tram tracks and hastened the end of the line. By then only two locomotives were left, No 7, the Manning Wardle of 1888, and No 5, the England 0-4-0WT of 1857.

On closure, the GWR purchased No 5 *Jane* and had it restored and placed on a plinth on Wantage Road Station. It was also fitted with the nameplates *Shannon*, the name it bore when first built in 1857 for the Sandy & Potton Railway. After the station closed in 1965 it was eventually moved to Didcot Railway Centre by the Great Western Society for restoration to full working order and appeared in the steam cavalcade at Shildon in 1975. No 7 was sold to a firm in Newport, Monmouthshire where it worked until 1958, when it was cut up for scrap.

Today little is left of the tramway, although the sheds and works can still be seen at Wantage and the office building in Wantage High Street.

Left: The Wantage Tramway Hughes 0-6-0 tram engine hauls its string of four-wheeled tramcars past a road coach, just north of Wantage Town in 1898. (*Lens of Sutton*)

Above: The Merryweather 0-4-0 tram engine shunts cars at Wantage Town in 1920. (*Lens of Sutton*)

Below: No 5 *Jane* and bogie car near Oxford Lane Halt about 1910, on the way to Wantage Road GWR station. (*Lens of Sutton*)

Above: The England (nearest) and the Manning Wardle locomotives at Wantage Town about 1900. The Manning Wardle 0-4-0ST No 7 has its original spectacle plate. Behind is ex-Reading horse tramcar No 5. (*Lens of Sutton*)

Below: Wantage Tramway No 7 shunts wagons at Wantage Town yard in 1935. The timber building in the foreground is the locomotive shed. (*Lens of Sutton*)

AN ACTUAL FACT
A curious race has come to pass.
Between an engine and an ass.
The Wantage Tram, all steam and smoke
Was beat by Arthur Hitchcocks moke

Sept 1923   ECF

Above: A famous commercial postcard cartoon which provides an interesting commentary on the speed of Wantage Tramway trains. (*F. J. Burgiss*)

Below: No 7 trundles a train of wagons and vans down to Wantage Road as a cyclist races by in June 1935. (*Lens of Sutton*)

Above: 0-4-0WT *Jane* at Wantage in 1925. This machine was one of the last original England products to see everyday service.

Top right: Manning Wardle 0-4-0ST No 7 shunting at Wantage Town in 1935. Note the cab has been re-built with an overall spectacle plate; the chain used for shunting wagons on the adjoining line would not be permitted today.

Right: The last journey of 0-4-0WT *Jane* to Wantage Road from Wantage Town in 1947. Happily, this machine was saved by the Great Western Railway and is now preserved at Didcot Railway Centre, Oxfordshire.

26 WOTTON TRAMWAY
The Brill branch

The Oxford & Aylesbury Tramroad was originally promoted in 1870–2 by the Duke of Buckingham as the Wotton Tramway to serve his estate and surrounding area. The change of title came in the 1890s when plans were drawn up for an extension to Oxford which never matured. The tramway, originally laid in 30 lb bridge rail, was opened to traffic on 1 April 1871 and ran from Quainton Road, on the Aylesbury & Buckingham line, to Brill in the Vale of Aylesbury. Originally the company owned two Aveling & Porter 0-4-0 geared locomotives which operated the line for the first decade or so before the Tramway purchased its first conventional locomotive, a Manning Wardle contractor's K type 0-6-0ST, named *Huddersfield*, in 1894. Between the arrival of the original Aveling machines the company briefly owned a Bagnall 0-4-0 tram locomotive, but it was not a success and was soon sold to a contractor.

For public passenger traffic the line also had a tram type four-wheel carriage, and a bogie vehicle with balcony ends. This latter vehicle had buffing gear of suitable height to couple with wagons of other railways in addition to internal user wagons owned by the tramway.

Stations and other buildings were simple wood structures with wood framing. It is believed that Colonel Stephens formulated many of his ideas for light railways after visiting the Brill branch on a number of occasions.

The company was never very solvent and on a number of occasions had to be helped out of trouble by Earl Temple, one of its benefactors. There were a number of occasions when Earl Temple had to pay bills to prevent creditors from closing the line.

In 1894 the company purchased a further Manning Wardle K type 0-6-0ST which later bore the name *Earl Temple*; a third Manning Wardle was named *Wotton* and carried the number 2 while *Earl Temple* was later renamed *Brill* and numbered 1.

Both the Aveling geared locomotives were sold in the late 1890s, going to a brickworks near Weedon, Northants. After the closure of the brickworks one engine was scrapped but the other survived and was later acquired by London Transport for its collection of historical relics. *Huddersfield* was used less after the arrival of the two Manning Wardle tanks in the early 1890s.

Left: One of the Aveling & Porter geared engines near Wotton about 1880. The Wotton Tramway owned two of these odd machines, one of which is now preserved in the London Transport collection at Covent Garden. At this time the GWR operated the Aylesbury & Buckingham Railway, with which the Tramway connected at Quainton Road, hence the GWR Dean four-wheel full brake on loan. Note the line's four-wheel carriage at the end of the train, behind the cattle vans. (*LPC courtesy Ian Allan*)

Above: The tram carriage at Quainton Road about 1886. This rather strange vehicle survived to be taken into the Metropolitan stock. Later it served as a grounded body at Brill shed until 1935 when, like the shed, it was demolished. (*LPC courtesy Ian Allan*)

In 1894 the tramway was entirely rebuilt. Track at Quainton Road and other stations was completely relaid with bullhead rail, and new platforms were built. From its opening in 1868, the Aylesbury & Buckingham line was worked by the Great Western. However after the Metropolitan Railway had reached Aylesbury the Great Western relinquished its interests in this cross country connection and in 1894 the Metropolitan, under Act of Parliament, took over the Aylesbury & Buckingham. The new owners soon put in hand improvements which included track doubling and rebuilding the station buildings between Aylesbury and Verney Junction.

The Metropolitan also took over the Oxford & Aylesbury Tramroad under a management contract. The new management was quick to get rid of the old tramway vehicles and replace them with Met standard vehicles, which included some rigid eight-wheel carriages, redundant from the Metropolitan's services in London.

The Metropolitan also disposed of *Huddersfield* to a contractor. Both the newer Manning Wardle tanks were retained and, after overhaul, reappeared on the line resplendent in Metropolitan maroon livery. Later, after the withdrawal of the Manning Wardle engines Beyer Peacock 4-4-0Ts, normally Nos 41 and 23, which with other members of the class had been displaced by electrification of the Inner Circle in 1905, were used on the branch.

The Brill branch, as it was now officially called,

served several small industries, in addition to the local farming community, including a brickworks near Wood Siding, and a small gasworks at Westcott. The branch continued to function as part of the Metropolitan Railway until 1933 when the Metropolitan itself became a part of the London Passenger Transport Board.

In late 1933 officers of the LPTB made an inspection of the Metropolitan system including the Brill and Verney Junction lines. As the special inspection train returned to Baker Street along the rural extension lines from Amersham, it was decided by London Transport not only to close the Brill branch but to hand over the line between Aylesbury and Verney Junction to the LNER.

The Brill branch closed to all traffic on 30 November 1935. London Transport had one further job to do before handing the line back to its owners for demolition, for the Tramway Company still existed on paper. This was to take out of service the points connection at Quainton Road and clip and padlock the switch blades, which was carried out the following day. Alas in 1935 there was no such thing as the branch line preservation. The Verney Junction line was closed by the LNER to passenger traffic in 1936 and to all traffic after the second world war.

Today little remains of the Brill branch. The Quainton Preservation Society occupies the station area at Quainton Road. This is the sole reminder of the line except for the GPO letterbox at Brill still marked 'Brill Station'.

Left: Metropolitan Beyer Peacock 4-4-0T No 41 starts out of Wood Siding in 1932 with a train for Brill. The Great Western Birmingham main line of 1910 passed under the Brill branch at this point. The 4-4-0T trails a former Metropolitan rigid eight-wheeled brake third. (*Lens of Sutton*)

Below left: One of the Manning Wardle 0-6-0STs, *Brill No 1* at Brill yard in 1901, in a coat of Metropolitan maroon paint. The two Manning Wardle tanks were the only locomotives kept by the Metropolitan after the 1894 takeover. The railway staff in front of No 1 are the entire Brill shed and station staff at that time. (*Lens of Sutton*)

Below: Wotton station and yard on the Brill Tramway in 1934. (*Lens of Sutton*)

Above: Brill station and locomotive shed in August 1935, only a few months before closure. Metropolitan 4-4-0T No 23 has already received LT lettering but retains its Met number. Later it became No L45 and today is preserved in the LT collection at Covent Garden LT Museum. Note the original wooden buildings of the Tramway Company with their clinker outer boards and rickety old water tanks. *(Lens of Sutton)*

Below: No 23 at Aylesbury station in 1935 with a goods train from the Brill Tramway. Once a week the A class 4-4-0T would travel from Brill to Neasden and the second 4-4-0T would be sent down in the opposite direction, often on a goods train, to relieve it. *(Lens of Sutton)*

27 PLA PASSENGER LINES
The Royal Albert Dock Railway and the Millwall Extension Railway

In the Port of London one could find a collection of interesting lines connecting the various internal harbours and jetties to the main line railways. In modern times these lines have largely been controlled by the Port of London Authority, but in the 19th and early part of the present century each internal dock railway was owned by quite separate dock companies. Two are the subject of this chapter, for they owned and ran two short independent passenger lines, which ran every day for the general public.

The Royal Albert Dock Co opened a line on 3 August 1880 from Albert Dock Junction to Central Station, worked at first by the London & St Katharine Dock Co. Trains ran from 8.30 am until 6.00 pm, half-hourly at first, later expanded to three trains an hour.

From 1881 Central station was no longer a terminus, and trains ran to the newly-built Gallions Station. The line had lower quadrant slotted post signals at intervals along the line, controlled by ground frames at each station. Permanent way was light with 45 lb rail on chaired sleepers. The line had a small fleet of three ex-LNWR Allan 2-4-0Ts with a collection of a dozen or so mixed four-wheeled coaches fitted with Clark and Webb chain brakes, which included former GER and LTSR vehicles, the only vehicles the line ever appears to have possessed. The Royal Albert Dock line closed to passenger traffic in 1932, but by this time the line was in the hands of the LNER under an operating agreement with the PLA.

Both the station buildings at Gallions and Custom House were brick and wooden structures built to main line standards; they were later badly damaged during the second world war by bombing. In later years the line was used only by PLA internal goods traffic. The original ex-LNWR 2-4-0Ts were withdrawn for scrap in 1896, after which hired GER locomotives were used, and, later, NER types. The PLA also had a large fleet of tank locomotives of its own for shunting its dock lines; some had vacuum brakes for working ocean liner passenger trains to Tilbury Docks, for which LMS stock was used.

The livery of the original 2-4-0Ts had been black with thin red lining and gold lettering, shining brass and copper work, and red buffer beams. Coaches were dark brown with grey roofs. The railway had no goods stock of its own but the PLA ran ordinary through goods trains to and from the docks over its tracks.

The second dock line had a rather more bizarre career and, indeed, it was a gem of minor railway history. The Millwall Extension Railway, only just over $1\frac{1}{2}$ miles in length, opened to goods traffic in December 1871 and to passengers in January 1872. Between North Greenwich and Millwall Dock station the line was to cross the property of the East India Dock Co. This company opposed the Millwall Extension plan in every way it could because it saw the potential development of rival facilities, but eventually the Millwall Extension Railway and the East India Dock Co settled their differences. The Millwall Extension Railway had been built primarily to open up port facilities in the Isle of Dogs, partly financed by the Great Eastern Railway and partly by the Millwall Dock Co. Under the original Act of 1865, the company's title was that of the London, Blackwall & Millwall Extension Railway, but ownership at first was shared between the London & Blackwall, the London & India Docks Co, and the Millwall Dock Co, each owning sections of line.

The station buildings were built of timber with simple platforms and shelters. The line ran over several viaducts on its way from North Greenwich to Millwall Dock Station, some of them flimsy timber affairs.

The railway ran a 'rapid' transit service with a fast turn round of only a few minutes but with horse traction, for steam locomotives were barred from the viaducts. Steam locomotives were used on the last few hundred yards into North Greenwich. From 1880, after some of the bridges had been strengthened, steam locomotives were used throughout, together with hired coaches. The steam locomotives consisted of a fleet of six Manning Wardle 2-4-0Ts. These attractive but underpowered machines ran the service on the line

Above: Millwall Extension Railway Manning Wardle 2-4-0T No 3 at North Greenwich about 1905 with a train of ex-GER four-wheel stock. Note the wooden buildings in the background. (*Lens of Sutton*)

Top right: 2-4-0T No 5 in pseudo Stroudley livery about 1901 with two ex-GER four-wheelers at Millwall. Unlike the other stations Millwall had a heavy brick building and platform, and had a GER stationmaster. (*Lens of Sutton*)

Right: The other Dock minor railway was the Royal Albert Dock Railway. This line owned some ancient LNWR Allan 2-4-0Ts and ex-GER four-wheel stock. The train is seen at Customs House in about 1902. (*LPC courtesy of Ian Allan*)

from 1871 until 1926 when it closed. The little tanks were fitted with bird-nest type spark arresters, and their livery was similar to LBSCR Stroudley yellow. The carriage stock in later years was ex-GER and ex-NLR, painted medium brown and with gold lettering and black roofs. It was a custom on the line to use the side tanks of the locomotives as advertising bill boards and posters were often stuck on them.

By the early 1920s the six 2-4-0Ts had become worn out and the PLA searched for new motive power, eventually purchasing three Great Western steam rail motors. However these machines, apart from being rather a tight fit in places, did not attract passengers, and were soon withdrawn. The little 2-4-0Ts returned but only for a short time, for on 4 May 1926 during the general strike, the footplatemen arrived at Millwall Dock gates only to be turned away by the dock picket. The railway never re-opened. The PLA and LNER had intended to close the railway from 1 July 1926, but the strike had brought this date forward.

Above: Allan 2-4-0T at Custom House station in 1900. The 2-4-0s were built originally for the LNWR based on an 1840s design, rebuilt as 2-4-0Ts in the 1860s and later sold to the Albert Dock Company. (*LPC courtesy Ian Allan*)

Below: The PLA took over most of the former dock lines after the first world war. Included in the takeover were the lines described, as well as the dockside goods section. PLA No 11 was an ex-Liskeard & Caradon engine, formerly named *Cheesewring* built in 1862, rebuilt by the Dock Board about 1920, and seen in PLA service in 1930. (*Photomatic*)

28 CORRINGHAM LIGHT RAILWAY

Built originally to serve an explosives factory, which in the first world war produced the explosive kynite, the Corringham Light Railway ran in an area of $2\frac{3}{4}$ miles from Corringham to Coryton, once called Kynochtown, in south east Essex just across an inlet of the Thames from Canvey Island. It was, moreover, linked with a siding connection to the Thames Haven branch, originally built in 1854 in the hope of developing a continental port for fish and cattle traffic. The Corringham line was opened by Messrs Kynochs in 1901, having obtained a light railway order in 1899.

In later years the light railway became the property of the Shell Oil Group which closed it but opened new sidings at Thames Haven. However the new owners still use Coryton Station and locomotive depot for storage of locomotives and stock.

The first CLR locomotive was an 0-4-0WT formerly owned by the Barry Railway, which worked both goods and passenger trains. Later a second locomotive, a Kerr Stuart 0-4-0ST named Cordite, was purchased for shunting traffic to and from the explosives factory. A third locomotive then arrived, an 0-4-2T Waterloo class locomotive, named Kynite after the explosive, built by Kerr

Stuart. Lastly the company purchased an Avonside class B3 standard 0-6-0ST in 1917. This released the 0-4-0WT for scrapping, and Cordite for resale.

At this time the railway possessed two toast-rack bogie carriages, which were later scrapped in 1920 when replaced by two ex-LTSR four-wheel vehicles. By the 1930s the CLR had obtained two former Midland bogie coaches, in addition to the two ex-LTSR four-wheelers. Bogie stock was no stranger to the line. In the first world war the company regularly had trains of Midland bogie coaches on ammunition workers services from London. These trains, in rakes of about ten to twelve vehicles, were worked by two locomotives, one at each end. The railway had no wagons of its own, and used main line vehicles which happened to be on its line for its internal needs.

Above: A rare shot of the first Corringham Light Railway Avonside 0-6-0ST, at Coryton with a train of Midland bogie stock during the first world war. These trains ran from Fenchurch Street to Coryton conveying ammunition factory workers in the morning and back at night. (*Ivor Gotheridge collection*)

The stations at Corringham and Coryton were substantial brick shelters with brick platforms, quite unlike structures of this kind on most other light railways of the period.

By 1930 the 0-4-2T *Kynite* had been discarded and stood at the end of a siding at Coryton, along with the ex-LTSR four-wheel third. From this time on two Avonside 0-6-0STs and the bogie were the mainstay of the line for in 1928 the company had purchased an ex-WD Avonside 0-6-0ST from the Shoebury Military Railway. Built in 1917, both it and its sister of class B3 ran the service until 1950 when the line was taken over by the Shell Mex Company and dieselised with two Ruston 0-4-0 diesel shunters.

The livery in the early days had been dark green lined black and orange for locomotives and, plain brick red for the carriage stock. By the late 1930s the carriage stock was turned out in light grey, and the locomotives in plain black.

The main part of the light railway closed to all traffic in late 1950, the track being removed in 1952. Today the station building still stands at Coryton, and the 0-4-0 diesels still shunt Shell bogie tank cars around the curve to the sidings at Thames Haven.

Right: Kynite passes a crude contractor's type distant signal near Coryton Jc in 1905. The signal has a simple hard lever and rod mechanism. (*Ken Nunn courtesy LCGB*)

Bottom right: Corringham station about 1920 showing the brick buildings and platform with its neat gas lamps (*Lens of Sutton*)

Below: The second Avonside 0-6-0ST of 1917 at Corringham in 1926 with a mixed train consisting of Midland bogie brake third, an LTS four-wheel third and ex GE 12T open wagon in front of the locomotive. (*Lens of Sutton*)

Above: Kynite and toast rack brake car at Corringham station in 1905 awaiting the road to Coryton with an afternoon train. (*Ken Nunn courtesy LCGB*)

Centre: One of the original toast rack bogie vehicles at Corringham about 1906, showing its open sided construction and tram type seats. These vehicles were withdrawn from service just before the first world war. Note the low sided dumb buffered open wagon with its top planks missing. (*LPC courtesy Ian Allan*)

Bottom: Kynite dumped at Coryton shed with other rotting stock in 1937. The carriage is an ex-LTSR four-wheel third; behind can be seen an ex-Cory Bros eight plank open wagon.

29 COLNE VALLEY & HALSTEAD RAILWAY

Connecting the Essex towns of Haverhill and Halstead to Chappel & Wakes Colne, junction with the Great Eastern line from Marks Tey to Sudbury through the Stour valley, the Colne Valley & Halstead Railway was one of Britain's larger independent concerns. The line opened in April 1860 but within five years, another GE line, from Cambridge, had reached Haverhill, where the GE opened its own station, and continued to meet the existing GE line at Sudbury to form a through cross-country route between Colchester and Cambridge. More important to the CV&H the GE had a parallel but longer route between Haverhill and Chappel, and moreover provided the link to the London main line at Marks Tey. A connecting spur was laid in between the two lines at Haverhill.

The Colne Valley originally owned two George England-built 2-4-0Ts named *Cam* and *Colne*. Later they were rebuilt by Fletcher Jennings at Whitehaven works. The CV&H then purchased very cheaply a second-hand former LBSCR 2-2-2 tender locomotive, built by Sharp Stewart in 1849, but it was well worn and in poor shape, and lasted

but a year or so. At this time the railway used four-wheel stock from a variety of lines including former Eastern Counties vehicles and second-hand goods wagons. Then came a Sharp long-boilered 0-6-0 tender locomotive. Between the mid-1860s and the late 1890s the railway bought about a dozen new locomotives, ranging from Manning Wardle 2-4-0Ts to a class of three attractive 2-4-2Ts, not unlike the GER locomotives of the same wheel arrangement. All three had names, *Hedingham*, *Halstead* and *Colne*.

In its later years its carriage stock was a hotch potch of seven old Metropolitan C&W Co four-wheelers, and three ex-District Railway bogie electric coaches from the 1901 experimental electric train. The stations were substantial brick and wood structures; they were always well kept and platforms were usually decorated with flower beds and tubs of plants.

The company originally had its workshops at Haverhill, but in 1908 they were moved to Halstead. The railway always had a high standard of workmanship, but heavy overhauls and

CVHLR 2-4-2T *Halstead* and train of ex-GER four- and six-wheel vehicles at Halstead in 1907. The coach on the end of the train is one of the vehicles purchased in the early 1900s. At this time all CVHLR locomotives had stovepipe chimneys. (*Lens of Sutton*)

142

rebuilding were always carried out at Stratford GER works or by outside locomotive building contractors.

The last locomotive purchased by the company was a handsome 0-6-2T, No 5 on the CV&H list. It was built in 1908 by Hudswell Clark of Leeds, and like the other locomotives and stock it had air brakes. CV&H locomotive livery was black, lined dark red, coaches were in dark brown, and wagons in light grey.

The CV&HR became part of the LNER at grouping in 1923 and most of its coaches and internal goods stock were scrapped, along with its older locomotives. However the 2-4-2Ts and 0-6-2T survived until the late 1920s. One of the rationalisation measures was the closure of Haverhill CV&H station which meant that Colne Valley trains used the former GE station. Moreover the Colne Valley line service was later integrated with the service via Sudbury and some Cambridge–Colchester trains ran via the Colne Valley line. The CV&H line finally lost its passenger service in January 1962 – even diesel multiple-units could not save it – and was closed to freight in 1965; apart from a few buildings little remains today. The parallel GE line was truncated at Sudbury and today runs as a dead-end branch from Marks Tey.

Right: Colne Valley Railway 0-4-2T No 1 at Haverhill in 1901. This unusual machine was briefly taken into LNER stock in 1923. (*Lens of Sutton*)

Bottom right: Nos 1 and 2 at Halstead in 1921. Originally No 1 had a stovepipe chimney, replaced just before the first world war. (*Real Photographs*)

Below: No 5 at Halstead in 1921, perhaps one of the most handsome of all minor railway locomotives. Note the Westinghouse brake and locally designed chimney. (*Real Photographs*)

Above: The principal intermediate station on the CVHLR at Halstead, showing the sharply-curved platform and signalbox.

Below: Haverhill station CVR and goods shed about 1900. This station was later closed after the line was absorbed by the LNER in 1923 and CVHLR services then used the GER station at Haverhill. (*Lens of Sutton*)

30   MID-SUFFOLK LIGHT RAILWAY

Perhaps one of the most charming, if not one of the most beautiful, light railways of all time was the Mid-Suffolk Light Railway, opened on 29 September 1904. At first the line ran only from Haughley, junction with the Great Eastern, to Laxfield, and then only for freight, but was extended to Cratfield in 1906.

The branch had its origins in a short section of line built without official sanction between Kenton and Aspall Road, just north of Debenham, in 1903. This section ran for one year only until incorporated into the Laxfield branch, during which time only goods traffic was carried. Passenger services between Haughley and Laxfield began on 20 September 1908 but the extension to Cratfield, which did not see a passenger service, was closed in February 1912.

The railway ran through some of the finest country in Suffolk. Its stations were small and primitive with corrugated iron buildings, but neat gardens. Platforms were of the normal high level and built substantially of brick and asphalt; each station had its set of oil lamps and locally made station signs.

The company owned a fleet of three smart little 0-6-0Ts, Nos 1–3, built by Hudswell Clarke. No 3 originally ran for a short time as a 2-4-0T with its front wheels uncoupled. All three locomotives were originally named, if but briefly, No 1 *Haughley*, No 2 *Kenton* and No 3 *Laxfield*. The names were carried only for a matter of hours at Hudswell Clarke Works, when the official photographs were taken. All three survived to be taken into LNER stock in 1923. Originally they were painted dark maroon with black lining picked out in yellow straw. Later the livery was simplified to maroon with yellow straw lettering. Before No 3 arrived, a Manning Wardle 0-6-0ST *Chamberlain* helped out on the line. Original plans envisaged only the purchase of one locomotive and a steam railcar, but the railcar did not arrive. The railway

MSLR 0-6-0T No 1 *Haughley* eases a mixed train of ex-Metropolitan four-wheel stock and open wagons out of Laxfield station in 1920. MSLR locomotives and stock were kept in immaculate condition with shining brasswork and polished paintwork. The vehicle at the rear of the train is an ex-GER four-wheel brake van. (*Ken Nunn courtesy LCGB*)

also had a set of six ex-Metropolitan District four-wheeled carriages made redundant by their original owner through electrification. Centre gangways were fitted for use on the MSLR. The livery of the carriage stock was dark brown, but it is possible that at first the carriages were the same maroon as the locomotives. Normally they ran in two-car rakes. These vehicles survived until taken over by the LNER in 1923, when ex-GER six-wheeled coaches replaced them. At that time the original three Hudswell 0-6-0Ts were taken away from the line and replaced by 0-6-0Ts of class J65. Later still, in early BR days, J15 class 0-6-0s and J69 class 0-6-0Ts operated on the line, and at times a class E4 2-4-0 tender locomotive appeared.

The MSLR also owned a small fleet of goods vehicles for internal use, mostly open wagons and some open wagon conversions with van tops. There were also three parcels vans, a passenger brake van, a goods van and brake van. Livery for goods vehicles was light grey with white lettering.

The line was originally laid in 56 lb Vignoles rail, later replaced with chaired track and bullhead rail. It was originally operated using the split staff system but in BR days this was changed to one-engine-in-steam working. The Mid-Suffolk was remarkable for the number of public and occupation level crossings, for in all there were 86 in 19 miles.

The line was also noted for being a Westinghouse brake line although not perhaps surprising since the Great Eastern, its larger neighbour, used the Westinghouse brake. Indeed with GE engines and stock on the line in LNER and early BR days the Westinghouse compressed air brake was retained until the end.

The shed was situated at Laxfield but was only used for minor repairs, and for heavy overhauls locomotives were sent away to Ipswich or Stratford works of the Great Eastern Railways. A second small locomotive shed stood at Kenton, but was hardly ever used.

After nationalisation in 1948 the line became part of the Eastern Region of British Railways. It had but a short time to go for on 26 July 1952 it closed to all traffic. By this time the line was one of only three sections of BR where unsuspecting passengers could travel in non-bogie carriages, former GE six-wheelers still being in use, the others being in miners' trains in South Wales.

Left: No 1 in a sad state, dirty and unkept at Stradbroke in 1923, shortly after grouping, with a train for Haughley. No 1 had a long chimney fitted at this time. (*Real Photographs*)

Below: No 3 approaches Laxfield outer home signal in 1920 with a train from Haughley. Note the shunt signal on a bracketed support extended from the post. (*Ken Nunn courtesy LCGB*)

Above: MSLR No 2 at Kenton taking water from the makeshift looking water tower in 1919. The MSLR owned three Hudswell Clarke 0-6-0Ts No 1–3. One received an LNER number in traffic, but the other two were towed down to Stratford GER works and cut up in the early 1920s. (*Ken Nunn courtesy LCGB*)

Below: No 3 as a 2-4-0T at Stratford works GER in 1919, awaiting a light general overhaul. This shot shows its Westinghouse brake pump and the works number plates. (*Real Photographs*)

Above: Mendelsham station MSLR in 1951. (*Lens of Sutton*)

Below: A J15 0-6-0 and train at Brockford in 1951, a year before closure. The buildings of corrugated iron, the gas lamps and the home-made name board are all very much a part of what light railways were all about. (*Lens of Sutton*)

31 SWANSEA AND MUMBLES RAILWAY

The Swansea & Mumbles Railway was opened as the Oystermouth Tramroad in 1806, at first as a street wagonway. On 25 March 1807 it started the first public passenger service using a horse-drawn dandy which ran until about 1826. This was not merely the first public rail passenger service in Britain but also, it is believed, the world. By the 1850s, though, the line was derelict, having suffered from horse-bus competition on the new Mumbles road; it was relaid in 1855, after which services were reinstated. Horses were still used, but in 1877 steam traction was introduced to make the Mumbles line the second steam tramway in Britain after the Wantage Tramway, and the first to use steam traction in an urban street.

The line ran from Swansea's Rutland Street to Mumbles Pier, a distance of $5\frac{1}{2}$ miles. It had a connection from Rutland Street via a long siding to the GWR at High Street station, and with the LNWR at Mumbles Road, near Black Pill, again via a short branch, although both branches were only for local goods traffic. From the late 1870s the line had a small fleet of 0-4-0Ts and 0-6-0Ts fitted with skirts for tramway use; they were of Hawthorn, Brush and Avonside manufacture. The locomotives hauled street cars, not unlike the ordinary horse cars of the period, double decked with balcony ends. This was not the end of horse traction, though, because two companies were involved in owning and operating the line at that

time, which generated considerable friction for the next two decades until 1896, during which time horses were still used on some services. The railway had a small collection of open wagons for maintenance work.

The whole network was electrified in 1929, although some unsuccessful experiments had taken place with battery electric cars in 1902. The new electric cars were massive double-deckers seating 106, were built by Brush and operated at 650 volts from an overhead wire. They were designed to work when necessary coupled in pairs. Unusual was the automatic block signalling system operated through contacts bridged by the pantograph of a passing car. Steam locomotives were retained after this for goods trains, but by 1936 a Hardy petrol tractor and later a Fowler 0-4-0 diesel locomotive had replaced all steam locomotives on the Mumbles line by the late 1930s.

A number of companies were involved in the Mumbles line at different periods but the Swansea Improvements and Tramways Co had as much involvement as any between 1874 and 1927 when it transferred its interest in the line to the South Wales Transport Co – a bus undertaking. But the tramway survived for another 33 years and closed to all traffic in January 1960. A few relics remain to show what the line was like and the local museum has a fair selection.

Above: An Oystermouth bound tram near Lilliput about 1901, with short wheelbase and bogie cars; the 0-6-0T has no safety skirts fitted, and note the wood back spectacle plate. (*Lens of Sutton*)

Left: An 0-6-0T and tramcars at Oystermouth in 1910, as passengers board the cars for Mumbles Pier. Note the adverts on the decency boards and the station building in the background. (*Lens of Sutton*)

Right: Electric cars at Swansea LMS station in 1937. The Mumbles cars were heavier than the average electric tram. These cars operated in service in their original condition until the early 1960s. (*Photomatic*)

Below: Mumbles Pier station in 1913 with an Avonside 0-6-0ST on loan, running round the tramcars. This shot shows the top of the cars and the cramped seating quite clearly. (*Photomatic*)

32 CLEOBURY MORTIMER & DITTON PRIORS LIGHT RAILWAY

The Cleobury Mortimer & Ditton Priors Light Railway opened to goods traffic on 23 March 1901, and ran from a junction at Cleobury Mortimer with the Great Western line from Bewdley to the Shrewsbury & Hereford Joint line at Woofferton. It possessed only two locomotives during its whole independent life, both Manning Wardle outside cylinder, 0-6-0STs, named *Cleobury* and *Burwarton*, which were taken over by the GWR in 1923 and survived in traffic until the 1950s.

The line did not have a passenger service until 1908, when the company purchased a rake of ex-North London Railway four-wheelers, used in service until the GWR takeover. The company owned a fleet of goods vehicles, consisting mostly of open wagons, and two brake vans. In independent days the livery of the stock was black for the locomotives and medium brown for carriages, while goods stock was light grey. Apart from local rural needs, the line served a stone quarry at Ditton Priors, which used its own locomotives, until it closed in the late 1930s. The line had the minimum of signalling and relied on the staff and ticket system of train control. During construction, a Hudswell Clarke 0-6-0ST named *Fleetwood* was used by the contractor. This machine was of the same basic design as the Easingwold No 1.

Stations were of wood construction, with short awnings, and platforms were built of sleepers. The buildings along the line had a uniform neatness in their design, which, in the early days, were always kept in immaculate condition.

In 1923 the company became part of the GWR and the two locomotives became GWR Nos 28 and 29. Both continued to work the line and apart from short spells in service stayed in the Worcester area until scrapped. No 28 was loaned to the NCB to shunt at Hafod Colliery in 1951.

In GWR days the Royal Navy established an ordnance depot at Ditton Priors. This line used its own diesel shunting locomotives. The RN depot was used to store shells and for this reason all steam locomotives had spark arresting chimneys.

In GWR days both former CM&DPLR locomotives were rebuilt from saddle tanks to pannier tanks at Swindon, No 29 in July 1924 and No 28 November 1931. The new owners also used Dean four-wheel passenger coaches on the line until 1938, when the line closed to passenger traffic. The GWR used the CM&DPLR's old goods stock, including the hand crane, to maintain the line for some years after takeover in 1923.

The GWR operated a number of classes on the line, ranging from 2021 class 0-6-0PTs to Dean goods 0-6-0s. After 1948, the line had one return working a day. In 1956 operation of the line was handed over to the Navy since basically it was Navy traffic that kept the line open, using RN heavy 0-4-0 and 0-6-0 diesel shunters, until 1966 when the line finally closed.

Top: A very rural scene at Ditton Priors about 1909 with a Manning Wardle 0-6-0ST and ex-NLR four-wheel stock. Note the rather unusual use of the four-wheel goods brake van on the passenger train. (*Lens of Sutton*)

Top left: Cleobury at Ditton Priors in 1910 with a mixed train for Cleobury Mortimer comprising ex-North London four-wheelers and open wagons from the Abdon Clee Quarry. In the background behind the impressive water tower is a line of quarry open wagons ready for the incline. (*Ken Nunn courtesy LCGB*)

Above: Burwarton station in 1908 just after opening of the line. The stations on the CM&DPR were timber with sleeper-built platforms and oil lighting.

Below: After grouping the GWR took both the saddle tanks to Swindon and rebuilt them as pannier tanks. No 28, formerly named *Cleobury*, is seen at Cleobury Town in 1930 with a mixed train for Ditton Priors. The train includes two GW Dean four-wheelers and a train of five plank open wagons. The original brake vans were still in use. (*Lens of Sutton*)

33 BISHOPS CASTLE RAILWAY

The railways I have covered so far are, in the main, unusual concerns, with some interesting and in some cases unorthodox operating methods. However, none of the lines could fall in the same category as the Bishops Castle Railway. Indeed, the Bishops Castle could aptly be described as one of life's accidents, but nevertheless a very pleasant accident.

It was opened on 1 February 1866 as the first part of a cross-country main line from Craven Arms to Montgomery, but got no further than Lydham Heath, a small station in the middle of nowhere, $8\frac{1}{4}$ miles from Craven Arms, where a junction took a spur to the south west for $2\frac{1}{2}$ miles to Bishops Castle. Although the opening celebrations were in great style all the enthusiasm turned to dismay only a few months after the opening when the original company went bankrupt. The railway re-opened in early 1867, in the hands of an official receiver, who was on the look out for a purchaser to take over the unremunerative concern. He was unlucky, though, and it was still in receivership in 1935 when it closed.

Early in 1877 the concern found it hard to pay its bills, and after a High Court hearing a Mr R. Marston of Ludlow and a sheriff's officer took possession of the railway. A group of roughs was sent down to remove a length of track near Horderley. After this the men made a fire and had something to eat before bedding down for the night. However, some of the group had other ideas; after a while they decided that no train could possibly run that night and all adjourned to a nearby public house. News soon reached the railway's manager at Bishops Castle. By this time the town's coal and other basic supplies were right down to rock bottom. A locomotive crew and guard were found. A locomotive was steamed and slowly, very slowly, it proceeded to Craven Arms. A gang of men re-laid the length of track, and in the small hours of the morning a train of all the empty stock was worked slowly to Craven Arms.

The locomotive returned some hours later with full wagons of badly needed provisions. The bailiff's men had taken their fill of ale by this time, and only when the heavy train of loaded vehicles passed near Horderley did they realise that something was afoot. Out of the pub, they stumbled but, too late, the train had already

Left: Carlisle storming into Lydham Heath station in 1934. What a wonderful sight it must have been on that hot summer's day. (*J. E. Kite*)

Above: A rare shot of No 1, the ex-GWR 0-4-2T, at work on the line in 1910. No 1 was used less in service than *Carlisle*, and seemed to elude the camera when in steam. It is seen near Plowden with a train for Craven Arms. (*Real Photographs*)

passed. A few weeks later, after much negotiation, the railway re-opened and the bills were paid. The company was always in a state of financial embarrassment.

The locomotives themselves formed a wonderful part of railway history, due partly to the company's financial state and partly to chance. At first the system had an 0-4-0ST named *Bee*, but this machine was sold very soon after completion of the line. It was followed by an 0-6-0 named *Plowden*, built originally for the St Helen's Railway, but this too was soon sold, in 1874.

Perseverance, an 0-4-2T was the next locomotive to see service with the company. Built by Dodd's of Rotherham in 1854 as an 0-4-0T, it was later rebuilt as an 0-4-2T by the Newport, Hereford & Abergavenny Railway. Later it was sold to the West Midland Railway, becoming No 227, and was then sold by the GWR to the BCR in 1870; later it was sold to the Wrexham, Mold & Connah's Quay railway in 1887.

In 1861 the company purchased two 2-4-0s named *Progress* and *Bishops Castle*. They were originally built by George England for the Somerset & Dorset Railway in 1861, and both

were scrapped by the BCR in 1905. Finally came the railway's last two locomotives, ex-GWR Wolverhampton built 0-4-2T No 567, designed by Armstrong in 1869, purchased by the BCR in 1905 becoming its No 1, and perhaps the most famous Bishops Castle locomotive, *Carlisle*, a beautiful 0-6-0 contractor's tender locomotive. Built by Kitsons in 1868 it portrayed, above all others, the real feeling of the Bishops Castle. Originally it had a four-wheel tender, but after many years acquired a standard GWR Armstrong six-wheel tender. From the early days BCR locomotives went to Wolverhampton works for overhaul.

At first the railway owned a rake of three four-wheel coaches but these were later sold to the Golden Valley Railway. Until 1924 the BCR operated a set of three four-wheel LNWR coaches fitted with the Clark and Webb chain brake after which the company purchased an ex-LSWR six-wheel brake third and an ex-Brecon & Merthyr four-wheeler. These last two vehicles were supplemented by an ex-Hull & Barnsley four-wheel composite coach.

In addition the BCR owned a collection of

interesting wagons, including GWR 'iron mink' vans, some decrepit open wagons, and an ancient hand crane and runner. It also had a short wheelbase ex-GWR 'toad' brake van. The locomotives were originally painted black with yellow lining, but later this was changed to Brunswick green without lining. All brass and copper was polished, and the locomotives were always well groomed. No 1 never carried a name. The carriage stock was originally painted dark maroon, later changed to medium brown. Goods vehicles were painted light grey with white lettering. Stations were a mixture of substantial brick structures and wooden buildings.

The Bishops Castle became one of the most neglected byways, with lower quadrant signals in drunken positions, its track overgrown and its stations looking tired and neglected, but its staff were dedicated and faithful to the end.

The line slumbered through the years until in the late 1920s and was nearly closed on a number of occasions. The people of Bishops Castle even formed a Bishops Castle railway defence league, but to no avail, for no-one wanted the line. A third attempt was made in the late 1920s to sell the railway to the Great Western, but this again failed.

Colonel Stephens had ideas about purchasing the line; he despatched Mr Austen, his assistant manager, to inspect the railway sometime in the early 1920s. When Austen returned he had much to say about the concern, most of it uncomplimentary. He told Stephens on his return, 'don't touch that railway, it's so bankrupt that when they want new sleepers they go into the woods and cut a tree down'. Stephens lost interest in the idea after Austen had made his dismal report.

The receiver decided to close the railway at the end of 1934, and after the usual procedures, the line closed to all traffic on 20 April 1935. After closure *Carlisle* was used on the demolition train, and No 1 was considered by a colliery as a shunting locomotive but after an examination was found to be too heavy.

All the stock was broken up at Craven Arms in late 1936 and early in 1937. Only a signal, one of *Carlisle*'s name plates, and a few small relics remain today. It is indeed a great shame that unlike one of the signals, *Carlisle* did not go to York Railway Museum.

Left: Bishops Castle station in 1905; a train simmers in the morning sunshine, waiting to leave for Lydham Heath, while station staff and local folk pose for the camera. (*Lens of Sutton*)

Above: A mixed train at Lydham Heath about to leave for Craven Arms; the coach is an ex-Hull & Barnsley all third, while the wagons include a private owner open, a GWR iron mink van, and an ex-NER meat van. At the head is an ex-GER four-wheel brake van and *Carlisle*. (*Photomatic*)

Below: Horderley station in 1934 showing the substantial brick building with rays of mid-day sun glinting on its roof. The platform looks derelict and the building dowdy and neglected. A year later, after the line closed, it was sold and later became a house. (*Photomatic*)

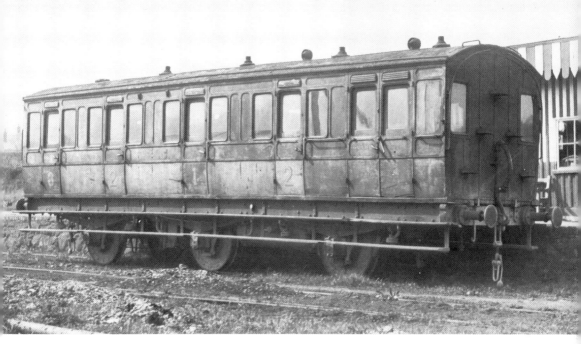

Left: *Carlisle*, was perhaps one of the most beautiful locomotives on any of the minor railways of Britain; it is seen at Craven Arms in 1910 with its original four-wheel tender. (*L&GRP courtesy David & Charles*)

Above: The ex-LSWR six-wheel brake tri-composite at Bishops Castle in 1934, in a tired coat of paint with worn paintwork and lettering. (*L&GRP courtesy David & Charles*)

Left: Bishops Castle No 1, an ex-GWR Armstrong Wolverhampton 0-4-2T of the late 1880s, here seen at Bishops Castle in 1930. (*Photomatic*)

Below: Wagons at Bishops Castle station in 1934. In the background is a train of old cattle wagons. In the middle foreground an ex-LNWR iron built wagon and a derelict looking match wagon. (*Lens of Sutton*)

34 MAWDDWY VALLEY LIGHT RAILWAY

The Mawddwy Railway was the creation of a rich eccentric named Sir Edmond Buckley. It ran from Cemmes Road between Newtown and Machynlleth on the Cambrian Railways main line, to Dinas Mawddwy, some 5¼ miles apart and opened on 1 October 1867.

The company possessed a collection of three old coaches; all came from different sources, one, an ex-West Midland vehicle, was an old parliamentary six-wheeler, while the other two were four-wheel coaches, one an ex-LNWR tri-composite first second and third class coach and the other an ex-Cambrian brake vehicle. The company painted its coaches in dark red, and its locomotives in lined olive green.

The stations along the line were in stone, of substantial construction, with oil lighting and shelters for passengers. There were hardly any signals and the line was worked by the staff and ticket system or one engine in steam.

The railway served a remote part of the Dovey Valley, and its main source of revenue came from farm produce. It made little money for its owner from the time it opened until in April 1908 it closed to all traffic, its passenger service having ceased in 1901. Closure, though, was only temporary. After four years dereliction the Cambrian acquired the line and reopened it in 1911. In 1923 it became part of the Great Western, which put up with its loss-making until 1931 when it too withdrew passenger services, continuing to handle goods with one train a day. In 1951 the Western Region finally closed it to freight traffic and the line was lifted during 1952. Today one can still find some remains of the bridges and the stations.

Latterly the line had been worked using Sharp 2-4-0 tender locomotives, with 2-4-0Ts in Cambrian days. In early GWR days 517 class 0-4-2Ts and auto trailers were used on the line, and later Dean goods 0-6-0 tender locomotives and small Cambrian 0-6-0 goods types were to be found. Latterly a Dean goods from Machynlleth worked freight services in the line's final years.

Above: A sketch of a Mawddwy Railway train with 0-6-0ST *Mawddwy* and two four-wheel coaches. (*Edwin Lambert*)

Left: Manning Wardle 0-6-0ST *Mawddwy* at Malwyd in 1900, with a train for Cemmes Road. Note the three link coupling with the vacuum hose at low level below the centre of buffer beams. The four-wheel coaches date from the 1860s.

35   SPURN HEAD RAILWAY

Built purely as a military line the Spurn Head was opened in 1910 to serve the naval lighthouse and lookout station at Spurn Head in the Humber estuary. In addition to its use in carrying materials to build the lighthouse, and to install a naval gun battery to protect the River Humber from surprise attack, the line had a limited passenger service for Royal Navy personnel.

The line ran over a long spit of shingle and sand from Kilnsea Fort to Spurn Point, a distance of about $2\frac{1}{2}$ miles. Apart from some simple buildings

Below: Spurn Head Railway Hudswell Clarke 0-6-0ST *Kenyon*, running as a 2-4-0ST in 1913. This locomotive ran during its lifetime as an 0-6-0 contractors engine and latterly with coupling rods removed as a 2-2-2ST. The coach is an ex-North London four-wheeler. (*K. Hartley collection, N. Redmayne*)

at Kilnsea Fort, the only significant building was the locomotive shed near Spurn Point, and the lighthouse itself. The gun battery stood on the north east side of the sand bar, between the locomotive shed and the lighthouse, facing out to sea.

An 0-6-0ST built by Hudswell Clarke was used in the early days, both to construct the line and later to run the service. In addition the Navy had several petrol railcars, among them cars built by Hardy, Hudswell Clarke and Drewry.

The LNER loaned several ex-NER 0-4-0Ts at different times. In order to transport these locomotives it was necessary to use a road flat trailer and tractor, for the Spurn Head line was physically isolated from all other standard gauge lines.

During both world wars, the line was used extensively, particularly for the movement of stores and naval personnel. After 1945, though, the need for the railway declined and the War Department closed the line in 1951. Track and installations were demolished soon after closure.

Far left: A rare shot of the famous sail trolley at Spurn about 1920; it was used to transport passengers on a regular basis over the line. (*K. Hartley collection, W. C. Harding*)

Left: The Spurn Head was physically isolated from the main line, and stock changes had to be done by road. This rare shot shows LNER Class Y8 0-4-0T at Patrington Yard on route for Fort Kilnsea. (*British Rail*)

Above: The Hudswell Clarke railcar at Spurn about 1928; after this vehicle arrived *Kenyon* was stored and later sold. (*K. Hartley collection, N. Redmayne*)

Below: The pre-1914 Itala car used as a makeshirt railcar on the line, taken about 1919. (*J. Codd*)

36 CAWOOD, WISTOW & SELBY LIGHT RAILWAY

The CW&SLR opened to traffic on Wednesday, 16 February 1898. The railway, which had been promoted by local people, ran from Cawood to Selby, serving a remote community in mid-Yorkshire and became a part of the North Eastern Railway on 1 January 1900. The three stations along the branch were substantial brick structures with all the trappings of modern late 19th century life.

The company spent so much money on construction that it had to hire its rolling stock from a stock company. Initially one locomotive, a Manning Wardle class L 0-6-0ST named *Cawood*, works No 1360 of 1897, was on hire. It was almost identical to *Banburgh* on the North Sunderland Light Railway. At times of stress the NER would provide the line with a suitable locomotive on loan. In addition to *Cawood* the CW&SLR hired a rake of three four-wheeled coaches. Sometimes the NER sent bogie vehicles down the branch on special excursion trains. At no time did the company own any goods stock of its own. After the North Eastern take-over the existing rolling

stock was hired for a short time, after which it went back to the hire company.

After *Cawood* had departed from the line the new owners used Class E 0-6-0Ts and an H2 0-6-0T with enlarged side tanks, No 407. The branch also saw several experimental railcars, including the NER petrol railcar and later an LNER railbus, one of which caught fire at Selby shed in 1926. By the late 1930s the line was operated by an ex NER 0-4-4Ts and a Sentinel steam railcar.

Regular passenger trains ceased after 31 December 1929, but special excursions continued to run right up to final closure on 2 May 1960, by which time the line remained open only for agricultural goods traffic, on a one return trip a day basis. These goods trains were operated by either ex NER J77 0-6-0Ts or BR 204hp 0-6-0 diesel mechanical shunters.

0-6-0ST *Cawood* at Cawood station on opening day with the CWSLR directors posing for a photograph. A year later the NER took over the line and *Cawood* was sold to a contractor. (*K. Hoole*)

37   DERWENT VALLEY LIGHT RAILWAY

The Derwent Valley Railway story is a happier tale than most, for unlike most of the lines in this book part is still open today. Moreover ownership of the concern has not changed since it opened. It is operated by a private company but BR appoints one of the board's directors. In latter years the world 'Light' has been dropped from the title.

The line opened on 29 October 1912 between Cliff Common and Wheldrake and was extended to York Laythorpe on 21 July 1913; it then connected at both ends with the NER lines at Cliff Common and Laythorpe. At first the DVLR hired suitable locomotives from the NER, normally 0-6-0Ts of various classes. During the first world war DVLR trains ran into Selby NER station,

about three miles west of Cliff Common.

For passenger services the railway owned a Ford back-to-back railbus set, not unlike those used by the Colonel Stephens lines; it was later sold to the County Donegal Railways Joint Committee where, after conversion to 3ft gauge, it ran for many years. The railway also had an 0-4-0 petrol tractor used for shunting and short trip working.

The DVLR was the first railway in Britain to purchase a Sentinel 0-4-0 geared locomotive, delivered from the Sentinel Works free of charge over the LMS and LNER, both of which tested it and decided to purchase their own fleets as a result of its performance.

The Derwent Valley Sentinel 0-4-0 geared steam shunter at York Laythorpe station in 1935, shunting wagons into the goods yard. The locomotive at this time was painted dark green with black shaded yellow straw lettering. (*Photomatic*)

In the early days DVLR locomotives were painted in NER green and lettered in yellow straw, but today locomotive livery is grey with red lettering. Carriage livery in the past was brown, but light green for the parcels vans after 1926.

Right from the start the DVLR's permanent way was laid in bullhead rail to the standards of branch lines belonging to the major companies, and in contrast to the tracks of many independent lines which used either lighter bullhead rail or light flat-bottom rail spiked directly to sleepers. The only signal on the railway was at Wheldrake, an ex-NER slotted post lower quadrant stop signal. Normally the line was worked by the staff and ticket system. Station buildings were a mixture of small brick and concrete structures at most of the important locations and small timber-built goods depots for freight traffic.

Originally the coaching stock consisted of two four-wheel ex-NER brake thirds, but after 1926 when the passenger service ceased the railway disposed of both the four-wheelers and the railbus set. The company also owned a small fleet of open wagons and some vans for internal use, plus a four-wheel crane and runner. In 1946 the DVLR purchased an ex-SE&CR six-wheel full brake parcels van, one of type distinguished with a 'birdcage' roof observatory, also seen on some North Eastern coaches of the last century, which found their way on to some of the independent lines in the North East. The SECR vehicle was withdrawn by the DVLR in 1967 and preserved on the Bluebell Railway. In the late 1960s an ex-BR four-wheel parcels van was used.

After nationalisation the system remained independent, relying on BR to supply motive power, normally a J72 0-6-0T or an ex-NER 0-6-0 J21 tender locomotive. Later BR hired a class 03 0-6-0 diesel shunter to the DVLR. In 1969 the company purchased two ex-BR Drury 0-6-0 03 diesel shunters Nos 2244, 2298.

In 1975 the DVLR returned to steam and acquired J72 class 0-6-0T *Joem*, together with a rake of ex-BR Mk 1 coaches, in order to run a tourist steam passenger service between Laythorpe and Elvington in the summer months, as an attraction to the many thousands of visitors to York. Alas it was not a financial success and after a few seasons the DVLR management decided to withdraw passenger services for the second time at the end of the 1979 summer season. Freight traffic continues on the Derwent Valley, one of the few independent lines with an unbroken history.

Above: The one and only signal on the DVR, an ex-NER slotted post lower quadrant distant at Wheldrake, seen here in 1924.

Top right: Colonel Stephens who managed or owned many light railways in his group of companies (see page 83) set an example when he purchased railbuses for some of his lines. The DVR also purchased a Ford set. Later in 1926 the set was sold to the 3ft gauge County Donegal Railways in Ireland, and after conversion to the narrow gauge they gave many years good service. The set is seen here about to leave the DVR York Layerthope station for Cliffe Common in 1924. (*Photomatic*)

Right: Wheldrake station shortly after the original end of passenger services showing the mock Edwardian Tudor style building and the water tower. In the background can be seen the wooden goods shed and a siding full of dumped stock which includes an ex-NER four-wheel brake third. (*Photomatic*)

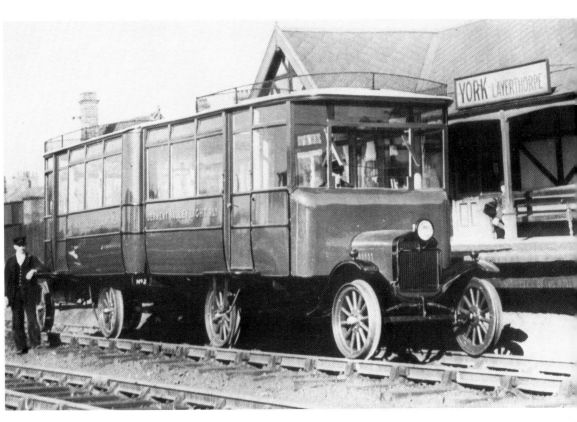

38   EASINGWOLD RAILWAY

Opened in 1891, the Easingwold Railway ran from Alne, on the North Eastern Railway's York–Darlington main line, to Easingwold, a small village only $2\frac{1}{2}$ miles from the main line junction. The Easingwold was locally promoted to transport agricultural and coal traffic.

The railway only had two main stations, at Alne where the line ran into a bay beside the NER platform and at Easingwold where the ER had its own small station and goods shed. There was a timber built halt at Crankley, near the level crossing, about $\frac{1}{4}$ mile north east of Alne. Crankley Halt also boasted a short siding for local milk traffic. The company hired and owned a number of interesting locomotives in its time. First was an 0-4-0ST built by Manning Wardle, originally used for contractor's work on the line, and later hired to the ER. This was replaced with ER No 1, a Hudswell Clarke 0-6-0ST built in 1891 and named *Easingwold*. This machine, which was owned by the company, was later sold to a contractor and replaced in 1903 by a new Hudswell Clarke 0-6-0ST, No 2, of a similar design to the first. In 1924 No 2 went back to the makers for re-building and

re-painting, during which time Hudswell Clarke loaned the railway an ancient 0-6-0ST named *Trent*, not unlike *Farmers Friend* on the Knott End Railway.

The carriage stock on the Easingwold originally consisted of two ex-NER four-wheelers, later replaced by two ex-NLR vehicles, but by 1938 the stock was down to a single ex-GCR (CLC) four-wheel brake third.

The railway had run a full passenger service of some eight trains daily in its early years but at the end it had shrunk to two return workings a day. The railway had no goods vehicles of its own, but relied on main line stock working on to the ER if wagons were required for local traffic.

The station buildings at Easingwold including the outside lavatory and the weigh house were built of wood. However the small locomotive shed was a brick building containing only one track for a single locomotive. Locomotives and coaches were painted dark maroon, but the coach colour was relieved by yellow straw lining and lettering. Locomotive No 2 ran in black, lined red, for a time in the early 1920s.

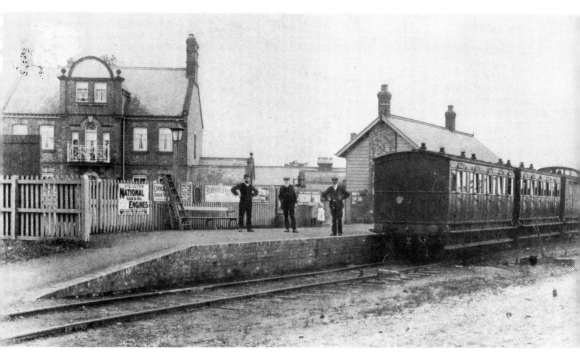

169

Left: A rare photograph of 0-6-0ST No 1 *Easingwold* at Alne in 1901. *Easingwold* was sold in 1903 to a contractor and replaced with a second Hudswell 0-6-0ST No 2 un-named. (*W. Horwood*)

Above: Easingwold station in about 1910 photographed from the buffer stops with locomotive No 2 and train of ex-North London four-wheelers including brake van in the platform. This is rather a good view of the back of the station with its fence festooned with enamel advertisements, and staff and children proudly posing for the camera (*Lens of Sutton*)

Below: Hudswell Clarke 0-6-0ST, ER No 2, at Easingwold in 1936. This machine continued in everyday use until 1947 when replaced by a hired main line locomotive. (*Lens of Sutton*)

The company scraped through the 1920s and 1930s until the second world war. The railway picked up for a time with some War Department traffic during the war years but this ceased in 1945. Passenger traffic though was poor and passenger services were withdrawn in 1948. Thereafter the company just about broke even every year until 1957 when it closed to all traffic.

Like the North Sunderland Railway the Easingwold was not nationalised in 1948 but carried on as a private concern. From then on BR provided the motive power in the form of an ex-LNER J72 0-6-0T. The Hudswell Clarke 0-6-0ST was stored for a short time before being sold for scrap in about 1950. The hiring of BR motive power went on until the end of the line's existence. With the help of BR the company's assets were wound up and the last train ran on 27 December 1957, after which the track was lifted.

Above: An Alne-bound train near Alne Crossing in 1946 with No 2 at its head. The Easingwold Railway hired locomotives from the LNER at times, including J71 and J72, 0-6-0Ts. The coaches used at this period were again ex-NER four-wheelers. (*Photomatic*)

Below: Two old carriage bodies at Easingwold in a rotting condition in 1957. There had been no passenger trains for eight years at this time but these are probably relics of the earliest coaches used on the line since they are not of North London or later NER type. (*Photomatic*)

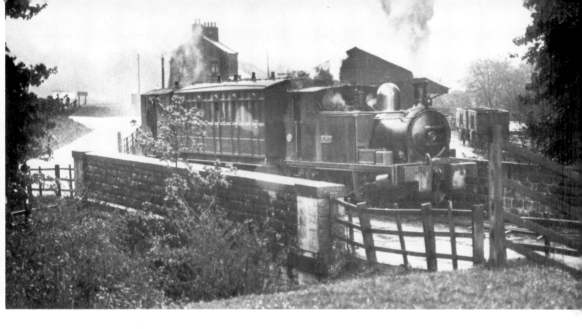

39 NIDD VALLEY RAILWAY

Built as a supply line to help in the construction of the Bradford Waterworks Nidd Valley Reservoir high in the Pennines at the foot of Little Whernside, the Nidd Valley Railway was opened on 11 September 1907 and ran from Pateley Bridge for seven miles up the valley to Angram Dam. The NER had exchange sidings at Pateley Bridge on a branch running south to Harrogate. Originally a line was planned with 2ft 6in gauge but this was abandoned in favour of a passenger carrying standard gauge railway.

Bradford Corporation owned a fleet of interesting locomotives which included examples built by Hudswell Clarke, Peckett, Avonside, Manning Wardle and Barclay, and two ex-Metropolitan Beyer Pecock 4-4-0Ts, overhauled and modified at Neasden MR works before despatch. The railway also had one ex-GWR Kerr Stuart steam railcar named *Hill*.

The carriage stock consisted of ten ex-Metropolitan four-wheelers and 12 ex-Maryport & Carlisle four-wheelers. At one time the railway also had a Hurst Nelson four-wheel private saloon but this was sold in 1910. Wagon stock was secondhand, mostly former main line stock from the NER and Midland.

The stations on the line were quite substantial for a long-term contractor's line, with heavily constructed brick buildings in some locations and timber built huts at others. The workshop and shed was at Lofthouse where all heavy repairs and overhauls were carried out. Despite its origins as a contractor's line the system was well provided with signal boxes and lower quadrant signals to divide the line into sections.

Angram Dam was completed early in 1935 and the railway closed a year later, but passenger services had ceased some years before at the end of 1929. Most of the locomotives were sold for further use to other contractors, and this even included the second of the former Metropolitan 4-4-0 tanks which although more than 60 years old went to Conway Quarry North Wales where it carried on working for a few more years. The other 4-4-0T and *Hill* the steam railcar went for scrap along with most of the other stock and equipment.

Nidd Valley 0-6-0T *Milner* starts out of Ramsgill station with a workmen's relief train, including an ex-Metropolitan coach, in the spring of 1928. (*Photomatic*)

Top left: Workmen's train for Angram Dam waits for the road at Pately Bridge in the early morning while its crew chat and pass the time of day. The locomotive 0-6-0ST *Blythe* and the stock Maryport & Carlisle. (*Photomatic*)

Left: A heavy goods train for the Dam blasts up the 1 in 50 towards Lofthouse in the spring of 1928 with locomotives *Milner* and *Gadie* at the head, with two unidentified Hudswell Clarke tanks at the rear. (*Photomatic*)

Above: The locomotive shed and works at Lofthouse in the summer of 1928 with *Hill* the steam railcar, and 0-6-0ST *Gadie* outside the shed. Note the stop signal and the timber boxed water tower. (*Photomatic*)

Below: Railcar *Hill* on the 1 in 50 in the spring, 1928. The attractive Yorkshire countryside makes an interesting contrast. (*Photomatic*)

40   GARSTANG & KNOTT END RAILWAY

Across the River Wyre from Fleetwood on the opposite bank stands the small town of Knott End, surrounded by marshland stretching for many miles. Until the late nineteenth century, this whole area was rather isolated, with only narrow roads leading out of the district. The only other way was the ferry to Fleetwood across the river. The local population, made up mostly of rural folk in a farming area, felt that they needed a railway to connect them more directly with the outside world.

In 1863 a survey produced a plan to build a branch from Knott End to Garstang connecting with the LNWR at Garstang & Catterall Station. The capital needed to build the line would have been £60,000 with debentures of £20,000. This would allow construction of the 15 mile branch along the mossy plain of reclaimed land.

The line had few features except a girder bridge across the Lancaster Canal at Garstang Town. As built the line was laid in lightweight 48 lb rail on longitudinal sleepers, but later it was replaced by bullhead rail on chairs on the main line and heavier flat bottom rail in the sidings and goods yards. It was opened between Garstang and Pilling on 14 December 1870, with a small 0-4-0ST named *Hebe* built by Hawthorn, and four four-wheeled carriages on hire from the respective builders. As the company did not have adequate funds the Garstang & Knott End Rolling Stock Company was formed in order to raise money to purchase further suitable rolling stock.

Hebe worked all traffic until 1872 when the original company went into liquidation. The company had overspent considerably during construction. The hired rolling stock was removed from the line and the formation was left to go derelict for two years until 1874 when a receiver was appointed to look after the former company's assets. The receiver purchased a new locomotive, a Manning Wardle Class C 0-4-0ST named *Union* and with this machine the railway re-opened to traffic in April 1875. At this time the receiver also purchased a rake of four six-wheeled balcony end coaches, two firsts and two thirds, the two firsts having upholstery. In 1906 two ex-Mersey Railway four-wheelers were added to stock but because of their bad condition were broken up at Garstang shed before being put into traffic. Indeed, motive power on the line came and went during the last 25 years of the old century. In 1875 the receiver had also purchased an 0-6-0ST named *Farmers Friend* built by Hudswell Clarke which was used on passenger trains while the Manning Wardle worked the goods trains. In 1883 *Union* was sold to Hudswell Clarke in part exchange for *Hope* an 0-6-0ST which outwardly looked very unlike *Farmers Friend*.

In 1897 another new 0-6-0ST built by Hudswell Clarke named *Jubilee Queen* was added to stock and in 1900 this was followed by a further machine named *New Century*. The earlier locomotives had been sold by this time. The Company owned eight

Left: A hearty beast indeed, GKE 2-6-0T *Blackpool* built by Manning Wardle of Leeds in 1909. *Blackpool* shunts carriage stock at Preesall Yard about 1912. Two GKE Manning Wardle engines survived to be taken into the LMS in 1923, but their lives were then short for all the Garstang's locomotives were cut up by 1925. Next to the locomotive, is one of the Knott End's attractive bogie saloons and a third class four-wheel brake. (*Lens of Sutton*)

Above: Hudswell Clarke 0-6-0ST *New Century* built, not surprisingly, in 1900 at Garstang Town station in 1910. This tank, together with *Jubilee Queen*, survived until 1925 at Crewe works LMS. (*Ken Nunn courtesy LCGB*)

Below: Garstang station about 1910, showing the yard, the locomotive shed, the station with its island platform and footbridge. In the foreground a group of permanent way men remove spoil from a tract of ground, probably after relaying sidings. (*Lens of Sutton*)

new bogie carriages with balcony ends, Nos 1–8, and two rather ugly four-wheeled brake vans Nos 9 and 10, all built by The Birmingham Carriage and Wagon Co. New goods stock consisted of both high and low sided open wagons and salt wagons with a solitary box van.

The railway was extended, at last, to Knott End on 29 July 1908, 45 years after the original plan was drawn up. By this time the company was solvent and owned its own rolling stock.

Station buildings were substantial brick affairs and Knott End, the terminus of the line, was quite impressive with two platforms and a central bay backing on to a brick building. At Garstang Town the station had an island platform with a bridge linking a footpath with the station. The line was

signalled with lower quadrant semaphore signals on wooden posts, worked from ground frames at each station.

The railway built a branch to Stalkine Moss in 1908 to serve a salt works. In this period in effect two separate companies ran the railway, the Garstang & Knott End Railway and The Knott End Railway, the latter operating the line from Pilling and Knott End. However the rolling stock was pooled between both companies and ran on both parts of the railway.

In 1908 yet another locomotive, an 0-6-0T named *Knott End* built new by Manning Wardle arrived on the line, followed a year later by a further Manning Wardle engine, this time a 2-6-0T named *Blackpool*, a large and unusual machine for a light railway.

Livery was originally black for locomotives and dark red for coaches, goods stock being painted light grey. Later, however, locomotives were painted in unlined red.

During the first world war the line carried heavy war-time traffic in addition to the large amount of existing agricultural traffic. However after the war ended services returned to pre-war levels and, soon after, in 1923 the railway became part of the London Midland & Scottish group. The new owners withdrew the balcony end bogie coaches and later sent them north to the Wanlockhead branch in Scotland where they served until 1939 when that branch closed. The locomotives received LMS numbers: *Jubilee Queen* became 11300, *New Century* 11301, *Knott End* 11302, and *Blackpool* 11303; both 11300 and 11301 were cut up in 1924 at Crewe, Nos 11302, 11303 following in 1925. After grouping an ex-LNWR steam railcar was used on the line as well as Class DX 0-6-0 goods locomotives.

In 1930 the LMS withdrew regular passenger trains, but special excursion trains still ran on the line in the summer months. In 1950 British Railways closed the line to goods traffic between Knott End and Pilling. The remainder of the branch was often worked by Ivatt Class 2 2-6-0 tender locomotives and, strangely, Stanier Black 5 4-6-0s on four or five wagon goods trains. Final closure came on 31 July 1963, and the track was lifted shortly after.

Jubilee Queen with a train for Knott End at Garstang Town in 1921. This shot shows the bogie cars and four-wheel brake van. (*Ken Nunn courtesy LCGB*)

41   SOUTH SHIELDS, MARSDEN & WHITBURN COLLIERY RAILWAY

Connecting the colliery town of Whitburn with South Shields this line had an extensive passenger and heavy coal train service. Stations were built at Westoe Lane (South Shields), Marsden, and Whitburn, for the pit.

The line opened in 1870 and from the start ran its own services with its own motive power. Station buildings were substantial brick affairs and at Marsden there was a three-road brick engine shed. Motive power came in all shapes and sizes, mostly ex-NER tender locomotives, and some old 0-6-0ST and 0-4-0T locomotives, mostly of Hawthorn build. The company used a small fleet of ex-NER, NSR and GER four-wheel coaches for workmen's and local trains. From 1910 part of the line at the Westoe Lane end was electrified at 575 volts dc overhead for shunting the coal staithes.

The journey took only five minutes on a passenger train and although intended mainly for colliery use the local people often used the trains as a convenient means of transport. By the mid 1930s the local buses had firmly bitten into the railway's

passenger revenue, and after this period only workmen's trains were run in the morning and evening. During the rest of the day coal traffic filled the timetable.

The system had ex-NER signals on lattice masts at each station. Overall livery for the locomotives, including the electrics, was black, while carriage stock was dark brown, though later light grey, and wagon stock was medium brown with black ironwork. The system came under the National Coal Board in 1947 and was closed completely in 1953. Although public passenger service ceased in 1946 trains for pit employees still ran and could be used by the public. Latterly the NCB used ex-WD 0-6-0STs on the line.

An ex-NER class J21 0-6-0, blasts a miners train of four-wheel stock up the bank out of Marsden Pit, towards Westoe Rd in the early 1930s. On the left of the train stand lines of ex-main line and private owner open wagons. (*Photomatic*)

Above: Class J21 No 7 hauls a heavy coal train up the bank from Whitburn Colliery in 1935. The company owned two ex-NER J21s, both purchased in the early 1930s to replace ex-NER 0-6-0 tender locomotives dating back to the 1880s. (*Photomatic*)

Below: NCB electric locomotives shunted the South Shields end of the line. Bo-Bo electric No 14 hauls a train of empty opens into Westoe Yard from Whitburn Colliery in August 1968. (*K. Hoole*)

Above: A rotting ex-GNSR four-wheel full third of the 1870s at Westoe Lane dump siding in 1935 awaiting its end. Note the wooden buffers and the guards platform seat and steps on the coach ends and roof.

Below: Ex-NER 0-6-0 No 6 at Whitburn shed in 1930 along with ex-NER J21 No 7 behind and 0-6-0ST No 3 in front. All the 0-6-0 tender types were withdrawn shortly after 1947 and replaced with ex-WD 0-6-0STs. (*Rev E. R. Boston collection*)

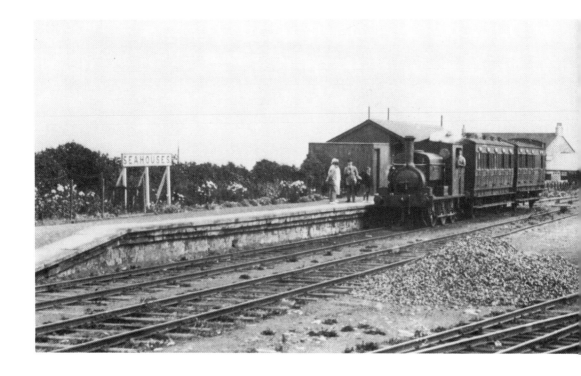

42   NORTH SUNDERLAND LIGHT RAILWAY

The North Sunderland Light Railway was opened to traffic in 1898. The line ran from Chathill, on the NER main line between Newcastle and Berwick, to Seahouses on the east coast, a distance of four miles, without intermediate stations. Station buildings at each end of the line were of corrugated iron and wood. The railway had no signalling and all trains were worked on the principle of one engine in steam. The line had a ruling gradient of 1 in 80 and was laid in light 45 lb flat bottom rail; later some of this was replaced with rail purchased secondhand from the NER.

The line was an early pioneer of diesel traction, and owned only two locomotives in its lifetime, *Banburgh*, a steam 0-6-0ST built by Manning Wardle in 1898, and a diesel mechanical shunter named *Lady Armstrong*. The locomotives had no shed and were stored in the open at Seahouses.

Before the diesel arrived in 1934 the LNER loaned the NSR ex-NER 0-6-0T No 407, and,

later, in times of need an LNER class Y7 0-4-0T even a Sentinel steam 0-4-0T and an ex-L&Y 0-4-0ST loaned by the LMS worked on the line.

The system had no wagons of its own, having to borrow goods stock from the LNER, but coaches came in three types. In early days the company had five ex-Highland four-wheelers, later replaced by one ex-NER four-wheeler and finally a pair of ex-GER six-wheelers. Five return trips a day were normally run with extra excursion trains when required. The company's carriage stock was painted light brown with black roofs and underframe, while *Banburgh* was in light green with red buffer beams; the diesel locomotive was black.

The NSR surprisingly was not included in the nationalisation plans of 1947, but in 1949 both its own locomotives were cut up and British Railways operated the line with a Y7 0-4-0T until 1951 when it closed completely.

Left: Seahouses station and yard in the mid 1930s, with *Banburgh* and train about to depart for Chathill. The goods yard seems pleasantly full of wagons and the staff will have plenty to occupy them in unloading the loaded vehicles. In the background is the locomotive shed; it was built for only one locomotive, which caused problems when motive power was hired from the LNER as the NSR's own engine had to withstand the harsh northern weather in the open. (*Lens of Sutton*)

Below: The NSR's only steam locomotive *Banburgh*, at Chathill station awaiting the arrival of the LNER connection in 1934 with a train of ex-NER stock. (*Ken Nunn courtesy LCGB*)

Above: NER 0-6-0T No 407 on loan to the NSR shortly before the first world war, here seen at Seahouses with a mixed train for Chathill. (*Ken Nunn courtesy LCGB*)

Below: Lady Armstrong stands in the platform with its train awaiting its passengers and the road out of Seahouses station. This notable little 0-4-0 diesel shunter was one of the first passenger hauling diesel locomotives in Britain. In the foreground a garden of beautiful flowers, grow higgledy piggledy in an unkempt rough flower bed, and the neat corrugated iron station buildings bask in the afternoon sun. (*Lens of Sutton*)

Above: Four-wheel open third at Seahouses on the NSR in 1937. This vehicle was designated as second, rather unusual for 1937. (*Lens of Sutton*)

Below: The North Sunderland Light was one of the first railways in Britain to use diesel traction, an Armstrong Whitworth diesel-mechanical shunter named *Lady Armstrong*, seen at Seahouses in 1936, with a train of four-wheelers consisting of ex-NER full third and the open saloon coach. (*Photomatic*)

43 CHANNEL ISLAND RAILWAYS

The Jersey Railway was opened in September 1870 as a standard gauge line and ran from St Aubin to St Helier, along the coast. Later an extension was built to Corbière, which served both the town and a local stone quarry. Originally the JR owned a fleet of five 2-4-0Ts, four of which were built by Sharp Stewart and one by Dübs, the latter later being sold to the WC&PR. Its rolling stock was a mixture of open-sided coaches and several closed vehicles. The railway also had a number or wagons, mostly opens for local freight and maintenance work.

In 1885 the company decided to rebuild the line using 3ft 6in gauge. This decision meant that new stock would be required to replace the existing equipment. A fleet of seven tank locomotives was purchased and a large number of four-wheeled coaches and wagons; much later two Sentinel steam railcars were acquired. In October 1936 a serious fire destroyed the station at St Aubin and most of the carriage stock went with the building. It was decided to close the line for it had been running at a loss for some years.

The Jersey Eastern Railway, opened in 1873 and built to standard gauge, ran from St Helier to Gorey. Its locomotive fleet consisted of four Kitson 0-4-2Ts, but carriage stock came in all shapes and sizes of four-wheel vehicles. By the mid 1930s this system had also acquired a Sentinel steam railcar, which after the railway's demise was sold for industrial use on the mainland. The carriage portion, though, is still in existence as a holiday bungalow on Jersey.

On Guernsey a tramway was opened in June 1879 from St Peter Port to St Sampson's. At this time steam tram locomotives, built by Merryweather and Hughes, hauled single-deck four-wheel cars. Later, bogie vehicles were introduced in addition to the original cars. In February 1892 the line was electrified using the overhead system, designed by Siemens Ltd, the Thompson Houston Co of the USA putting up most of the finance to convert the line.

It was one of the first electric tramways in the British Isles; after the first world war it made little profit and the management decided to close it to all traffic on 6 June 1934.

The last British-built line in the Channel Islands has a curious history. Built in early 1847, and opened in July of that year to serve a refuge

Left: 2-4-0T *St Heliers* and train at St Aubyn station about 1925 on the 3ft 6in gauge Jersey Railway. Behind the locomotive can be seen an interesting collection of bogie and four-wheel stock. (*Real Photographs*)

Above: Jersey Eastern Railway standard gauge 0-4-2T *Calvados* shunts stock at St Helier yard about 1900. The tank locomotive has an ornate lined livery and large circular windows. (*LPC courtesy Ian Allan*)

Below: A Jersey Eastern Railway slotted signal still in use in the early 1900s. Note the spectacle at the outer end of the arm to give the red, danger, indication. When the arm was lowered it uncovered the lamp to give a white, clear, light. (*LPC courtesy Ian Allan*)

harbour, the Alderney Railway was constructed for admiralty use. It runs between Mannez Quarry and Braye Bay, where it runs on to a breakwater built from stone produced from several quarries along the coast. Over the years the railway has had a variety of interesting locomotives and stock, including several Manning Wardle 0-6-0STs and 0-4-0STs. During the war the Germans ripped up the line and cut up the then surviving two Manning Wardle tanks. For a time a Sentinel 0-4-0T named *Molly* ran on the line. In 1958 this was replaced with a Ruston 0-4-0 diesel shunter which still runs on Alderney today.

During the war the German army built a number of narrow gauge military light railways on Jersey, Guernsey and Alderney. On Jersey two lines were built, one of metre gauge and the other of 60cm gauge. On Guernsey another 60cm gauge line existed, and there was also one on Alderney. After the Channel Islands were liberated in 1945 the German military railways were abandoned and later torn up for scrap. Only the Alderney breakwater line survives from all the interesting Island lines and as this book goes to press a tourist steam service has started.

Above: Jersey Railway opulence; four-compartment bogie first class coach No 12, built by the Bristol Wagon Works Co in 1887. (*Edwin Lambert*)

Below: An unusual four-wheel first and second class brake at St Helier carriage shed in 1920. Notable are the curved windows in the first class compartment, and a letter box (*Ken Nunn courtesy LCGB*)

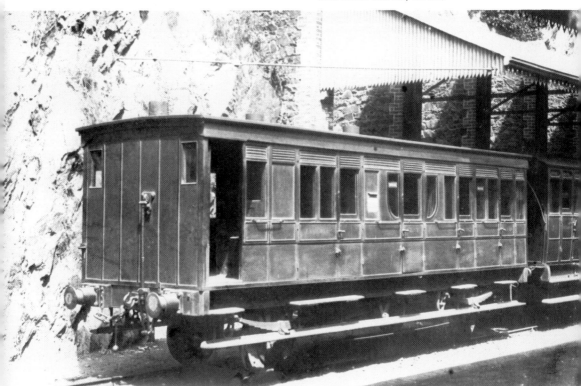

Above: Jersey Railway 3ft 6in gauge 2-4-0T and train arrives at St Aubyn station in 1911. This picture clearly shows this attractive part of the line along the coast. (*Lens of Sutton*)

Below: Jersey Railway 2-4-0T No 2 simmers at St Brelades terminus in the summer of 1930, while a group of people pose for a photograph. By this time the railway was becoming very dated in its outward appearance. By 1936 the railway seen here had been replaced by buses. Indeed the Jersey Railway Company still runs the buses today.

Above: Locomotive No 1 of the Alderney Railway, built by Hunslet of Leeds, Works No 231 of 1880, seen here with typical wagons in 1900. (*Edwin Lambert*)

Below: A Jersey Eastern Railway train arrives at La Rocque station in 1912. There is so much of interest in this view including the four-wheel vehicles, the brick buildings, enamel signs, and passengers in dress of the period. (*Lens of Sutton*)

Bibliography

Oakwood Press books:
Light Railway Handbooks 1, 2, 3, 5, R.W. Kidner
The Weston, Clevedon & Portishead Light Railway, C. Maggs
The East Kent Railway, A.R. Catt
The Ashover Light Railway, K. Plant
The Kent & East Sussex Railway, S. Garratt
The Plymouth, Devonport & South Western Junction Railway, A.J. Cheeseman
Festiniog Railway, Vols 1 and 2, J.I.C. Boyd
Southern Branches in the 1930s, R.W. Kidner
The Mid Suffolk Light Railway, M. Comfort
The Garstang & Knott End Railway, M. Price & R. Rush
The Liskeard & Looe Railway & Canal, L. Popplewell
The Brill Tramway, K. Jones
The Lambourn Valley Light Railway, R.C. Price
The Nidd Valley Light Railway, D.J. Croft
The Jersey and Jersey Eastern Railways, N.R.P. Bonsor
The Guernsey Railway, N.R.P. Bonsor

Industrial Railway Society books:
The Shropshire & Montgomeryshire Light Railway, E. Tonks
Snailbeach District Railway, E. Tonks
The Edge Hill Light Railway, E. Tonks

Other publications:
Light Railways of England 1900 - 1939, George Woodcock (Goose Publishing)
London's Lost Railways, C. Klapper
The Welsh Highland Railway, Charles E. Lee (David & Charles)
The Selsey Tramway, E.C. Griffith (privately published)
The Hawkhurst Railway, R.W. Crombleholme
The Bishops Castle Railway, E.C. Griffith (privately published)
The Mawddwy Light Railway, L. Cozens

Other sources:
Railway Magazine, 1899-1979
Great Western Railway Magazine
Willias Journal, The West London Industrial Archaeological Society
Welsh Highland Railway Society publications
The PLA Railways, collection of private papers
The Colne Valley & Halstead Railway, collection of private papers
Private papers in the collections of the Railway Club,
Narrow Gauge Railway Society, M. South, C.C. Green, E.C. Griffith
Public Record Office, BTC Railway Archives

Acknowledgements

I should like to thank the following people and organisations who helped in providing information and illustrations for the original two volumes:

The Tenterden Railway Company; Custodians of the W.H. Austen collection of photographs and data; Ian Allan (for LPC photographs); the Locomotive Club of Great Britain for the Ken Nunn collection; Lens of Sutton; Gregory Pictures; Mr Childs of the Clay Cross Company; *Punch* magazine; Real Photographs Co; W.H. Austen; J. Norris; F.H. Smith; D.A. Boreham; I. Gotheridge; H.C. Casserley; Charles E. Lee; E.C. Griffith; D. Cobbe; D. Kevann; P. Lemmey; J.E. Kite; J.L. Smith; P. Rowledge; K. Hoole; K. Hartley; C.C. Green; Photomatic Ltd; Real Photographs Ltd; H. Hopwood collection; British Rail; W. Hopwood; H.C. Casserley; and S.A. Henderson

I should like to give special acknowledgement to Robert Inns who through thick and thin has helped me by producing copies of excellent quality from old historic photographs, often at times from very poor originals. Also at this point I should like to pay tribute to the late Charles Kentsley who throughout his lifetime supported preservation and documentation of all railways large and small. Without Charles' backing and enthusiasm I doubt whether I should have started researching the railways of Colonel Stephens and hence written my first volume on this subject. It is a great shame that he did not live to see this volume published.